THE CHILD'S WORLD®

ENCYCLOPEDIA
of BASEBALL

WILLIE MAYS

VOLUME 3: REGGIE JACKSON THROUGH OUTFIELDER

By James Buckley, Jr., David Fischer, Jim Gigliotti, and Ted Keith

KEY TO SYMBOLS

Throughout *The Child's World® Encyclopedia of Baseball*, you'll see these symbols. They'll give you a quick clue pointing to each entry's general subject area.

Active player *Baseball word or phrase* *Hall of Fame* *Miscellaneous* *Ballpark* *Team*

The Child's World
www.childsworld.com

Published in the United States of America by The Child's World®
1980 Lookout Drive, Mankato, MN 56003-1705
800-599-READ • www.childsworld.com

ACKNOWLEDGMENTS

The Child's World®: Mary Berendes, Publishing Director

Produced by Shoreline Publishing Group LLC
President / Editorial Director: James Buckley, Jr.
Cover Design: Kathleen Petelinsek, The Design Lab
Interior Design: Tom Carling, carlingdesign.com
Assistant Editors: Jim Gigliotti, Zach Spear

Cover Photo Credits: Getty Images (main); National Baseball Hall of Fame Library (inset)
Interior Photo Credits: AP/Wide World: 5, 8, 9, 14, 15, 16, 17, 20, 21, 23, 24, 26, 27, 30, 32, 33, 36, 37, 42, 43, 44, 45, 46, 47, 50, 52, 56, 57, 59, 61, 62, 63, 64, 65, 66, 70, 72, 74, 75, 78, 79, 80, 83, 75; Corbis: 18, 22, 37, 39; Focus on Baseball: 7t, 10, 11, 29, 34, 35, 38, 40, 41, 49, 51, 55, 58, 67, 69, 71, 76, 81; Getty Images: 54; iStock: 31, 53; Al Messerschmidt: 12, 48; National Baseball Hall of Fame Library: 6, 7b, 28, 36, 68; Shoreline Publishing Group: 13, 19, 25, 60.

LIBRARY OF CONGRESS CATALOG-IN-PUBLICATION DATA

The Child's World encyclopedia of baseball / by James Buckley, Jr. ... [et al.].
    p. cm. — (The Child's World encyclopedia of baseball)
  Includes index.
  ISBN 978-1-60253-167-3 (library bound : alk. paper)—ISBN 978-1-60253-168-0 (library bound : alk. paper)—ISBN 978-1-60253-169-7 (library bound : alk. paper)—ISBN 978-1-60253-170-3 (library bound : alk. paper)—ISBN 978-1-60253-171-0 (library bound : alk. paper)
  1. Baseball—United States—Encyclopedias, Juvenile. I. Buckley, James, 1963- II. Child's World (Firm) III. Title. IV. Series.

GV867.5.C46 2009
796.3570973—dc22

2008039461

■ *The great Christy Mathewson.*

P EOPLE HAVE BEEN PLAYING BASEBALL, America's national, pastime, for more than 150 years, so we needed a lot of room to do it justice! The five big volumes of *The Child's World' Encyclopedia of Baseball* hold as much as we could squeeze in about this favorite sport.

The Babe. The Say-Hey Kid. The Splendid Splinter. Rapid Robert. Hammerin' Hank. You'll read all about these great players of yesterday. You'll also learn about your favorite stars of today: Pujols, Jeter, Griffey, Soriano, Santana, Manny, and Big Papi. How about revisiting some of baseball's most memorable plays and games? The Shot Heard 'Round the World. The Catch. The Grand-Slam Single. You'll find all of these—and more.

Have a favorite big-league team? They're all here, with a complete history for each team that includes its all-time record.

Ever wonder what it means to catch a can of corn, hit a dinger, or use a fungo? Full coverage of baseball's unique and colorful terms will let you understand and speak the language as if you were born to it.

This homegrown sport is a part of every child's world, and our brand-new encyclopedia makes reading about it almost as fun as playing it!

■ *Yankees hero Derek Jeter.*

Contents: Volume 3: Reggie Jackson ›› Outfielder

■ *Mighty Reggie Jackson swings for the fences.*

Jackson, Reggie

Outfielder Reggie Jackson was one of the game's biggest stars throughout the 1970s and into the 1980s. He was a famed power hitter known for his massive talent, big ego, and a reputation for coming through in the clutch.

Born near Philadelphia, Jackson starred at Arizona State in both football and baseball, and reached the Major Leagues with the Oakland A's in 1967. In 1969, Jackson hit 37 home runs by the midseason All-Star break, fueling talk that he might challenge Roger Maris' record of 61 homers in a season, set in 1961. But Jackson cooled off in the second half, finishing with 47 homers.

In 1971, Jackson hit one of the most famous home runs in baseball history, a towering drive that smashed off a light tower atop Detroit's Tiger Stadium during the 1971 All-Star Game. That same season, he helped the A's to the first of five straight A.L. West titles. Though they lost in the playoffs in 1971, they won the next three World Series. With great pitching, and led by Jackson's power, the A's were the first team to win three straight titles since the New York Yankees won five in a row from 1949–1953. Jackson was named A.L. MVP in 1973 and also won World Series MVP honors that year. After being traded to Baltimore and playing the 1976 season there, Jackson signed a record-breaking, five-year free-agent contract worth almost $3 million with the Yankees before the 1977 season. Though not large by today's standards, at the time, that was an enormous amount of money.

Right from the start, Jackson got into arguments with teammates, manager Billy

Martin, and owner George Steinbrenner. In one famous incident, Jackson got into a fight with Martin in the dugout at Fenway Park. However, Jackson helped carry the Yankees to the World Series. Against the Dodgers, Jackson hit a record five home runs, including a record-tying three—on three pitches, off three different pitchers—in the clinching Game Six, earning Series MVP honors for the second time. He got his nickname of "Mr. October" for his World Series heroics. He and the Yankees repeated their title in 1978, as Jackson batted .417 with four homers and 14 RBI in 10 playoff games.

Jackson signed with the Angels before the 1982 season. He helped the Angels win two division titles, bringing his career total to 11, and he also reached 500 home runs for his career. He retired after the 1987 season and was elected to the Hall of Fame in 1993.

■ *Jackson's fame inspired this candy bar.*

Jackson, "Shoeless" Joe

Please see page 6.

Japan, Baseball in

Baseball debuted in Japan in the 19th century and grew enormously popular thanks in part to the visits of Major League players. Ty Cobb led a tour in 1928. Babe Ruth and Lou Gehrig led tours of players in the 1930s. After World War II, professional baseball exploded in popularity in Japan. Currently, the Nippon Professional League is the country's version of the Major Leagues. Teams play in either the Central League or the Pacific League. The winners of those two leagues meet in a championship series, similar to the World Series, each fall.

Japanese baseball puts more focus on speed and bunting than on home runs. Japanese pitchers also throw many more pitches than in U.S. leagues. Practices are famously long and hard. The few Americans who have played or managed there have all reported on both the players' hard work and love for the game.

The greatest Japanese player of all time is generally considered to be Sadaharu Oh, who hit 868 home runs in his career, 106 more than the Major League record holder, Barry Bonds.

In 1995, Hideo Nomo went from Japan to the Los Angeles Dodgers and became a sensation, paving the way for players to

Jackson, "Shoeless" Joe

Joe Jackson was one of the greatest hitters of all time, but he was banned for life in 1920 after it was determined that he took money from gamblers to help throw— or lose on purpose—some games in the 1919 World Series.

Jackson grew up in South Carolina, and while playing a game there one day, he took his cleats off because they were hurting his feet. Fans began calling him "Shoeless Joe," and the nickname stuck.

■ *Jackson's valuable "Black Betsy" bat.*

Jackson reached the Major Leagues in 1908 with the Philadelphia Athletics, but it wasn't until he was traded to Cleveland for the 1910 season that his career began to take off. In 1911, Jackson, playing outfield, hit .408 in his first full season, which still ranks as the sixth-highest single-season average in modern Major League history.

In 1915, Jackson was traded to the White Sox, with whom he continued to star as one of the game's premier hitters. In 1917, he led the White Sox to the World Series title. Two years later, he batted .351 and drove in 96 runs, helping the White Sox to the American League pennant. The heavily favored White Sox lost the World Series to the Cincinnati Reds, and rumors began swirling that several players may have lost the games on purpose. Though Jackson seemed to be playing on the level—he hit .375 and didn't commit an error—he admitted the next year that he had taken money from gamblers. Jackson and seven of his teammates, known as the Black Sox, were suspended from baseball for life during the 1920 season. He never played in the Major Leagues again. Because of his banishment, Jackson remains ineligible for the Hall of Fame, even though his .356 batting average is the third highest of all-time. He died in 1951.

come to the Majors. Among the famous Japanese players in the big leagues are Hideki Matsui, Daisuke Matsuzaka, and Ichiro Suzuki.

Jenkins, Ferguson

Jenkins was born in Canada, and reached the Major Leagues with the Philadelphia Phillies in 1963. In 1966, he was traded to the Chicago Cubs and soon developed into one of the best pitchers in the game. Beginning in 1967, Jenkins began a run of six straight seasons of at least 20 wins, including 1971, when he won 24 games and the Cy Young Award.

Jenkins was traded to the Texas Rangers in 1974 and won a career-high 25 games. In his 18-year career, he led his league in wins twice and complete games nine times. He retired with a 284 wins and 3,192 strikeouts. In 1991, he became the first Canadian to be elected to the baseball Hall of Fame.

Jeter, Derek

Jeter grew up wanting to be the shortstop for the New York Yankees, and his wish came true. Born in New Jersey but raised in Michigan, Jeter had a great high school career, and was drafted by the Yankees with the sixth pick in 1992. He reached the Majors to stay at age 21 in 1996, winning the A.L. Rookie of the Year Award and leading the Yankees to their first World Series title in 19 years.

■ *Jeter is one of today's most popular players.*

Between 1998 and 2000, Jeter was the biggest star on Yankees teams that won three straight World Series titles. In 2000, he became the first and only player to win All-Star Game MVP and World Series MVP in the same season. Jeter has played in nine All-Star Games, won three Gold Gloves, and earned a reputation as a clutch player who has made some of the most famous plays in recent history. In the 2000 World Series, Jeter earned the nickname "Mr. November" for hitting a walk-off home run in Game Four. It was the first Major League game ever played in the month of November.

Jeter amassed 2,523 hits from 1996 to 2008, the most in baseball in that span. He played in the postseason 12 years in a row beginning in '96.

Johnson, Ban

 Ban Johnson was the founder and first president of the American League. For most of the 19th century, the National League, formed in 1876, was the dominant league in baseball. Other leagues, notably

■ *Randy Johnson shows off his power arm.*

the American Association, challenged the N.L. for supremacy but none managed to stick around. In 1901, Johnson, a former newspaper sports editor and president of a minor league known as the Western League, founded the American League through a combination of expansion teams and minor-league franchises. He wanted his new league to compete at the same level as the National League, and his new owners succeeded in raiding talent from the N.L., helping the A.L. gain traction in the national consciousness. In 1903, the modern World Series debuted, pitting the American League champion against the National League champion. Johnson died in 1931 and was elected to the Hall of Fame in 1937.

Johnson, Randy

Randy Johnson is a hard-throwing, 6-foot 10-inch (1.8 m) left-handed pitcher who has won five Cy Young Awards in his 20-year career. Johnson grew up in California and pitched at USC before reaching the Major Leagues in 1989 with the Montreal Expos. At the time, he was the tallest player in Major-League history, but he was more known for his wildness than his talent.

Blessed with a fearsome fastball that occasionally topped 100 miles (160 km) per hour, as well as an outstanding slider, Johnson, nicknamed "The Big Unit," made the first of 10 All-Star teams in 1990, the same year he pitched his first no-hitter. But it wasn't until 1995 that Johnson began dominating hitters. That season, he won the AL Cy Young award with an 18–2 record, a 2.48 ERA, and 294 strikeouts. He helped the Seattle Mariners reach the postseason for the first time.

Johnson was traded to the Houston Astros during the 1998 season and posted a stellar 10–1 mark with a 1.28 ERA. After the season, he stayed in the N.L., signing with the Diamondbacks. In Arizona, he had arguably the best run of any pitcher in history, winning four consecutive N.L. Cy Young Awards. In 2001, Johnson tied a record with three wins in the World Series, including the clinching Game Seven, when he came out of the bullpen to help stymie the New York Yankees long enough to allow the Diamondbacks to score two ninth-inning runs to win the Series.

In 2004, Johnson threw a perfect game against the Atlanta Braves. He joined the Yankees for the 2005 and 2006 seasons, but returned to the Diamondbacks in 2007. In 2008, he moved into second place on the Major Leagues' all-time strikeout list. By the end of the 2008 season, Johnson was just five wins shy of joining the exclusive 300-win club. With those achievements, The Big Unit looks like a lock for eventual election to the Hall of Fame.

■ *One of baseball's best: Walter Johnson.*

Johnson, Walter

"The Big Train," Walter Johnson, is considered by many to be the best pitcher of all time. Thanks mostly to a fastball that exceeded 100 miles (160 km) per hour, he won 416 games, the second most

■ *Chipper Jones is a former N.L. MVP.*

ever. He had a 2.16 ERA and a record 110 shutouts in his 21-year career, all with the Washington Senators. Johnson also struck out 3,508 batters, which stood as a record until 1983. He won 20 or more games 12 times, including 10 seasons in a row from 1910 through 1919, and he had two 30-win seasons. In 1924, he guided the formerly hapless Senators to their first A.L. pennant, then won the clinching Game Seven of the World Series. The Senators returned to the Series the next season as well, only to lose to the Pittsburgh Pirates despite Johnson's

two wins and 2.08 ERA. Johnson was also a terrific batter who hit .433 in 1925. He retired after the 1927 season. In 1929, he began his big-league managerial career, which lasted until 1935.

Baseball boasted many outstanding pitchers in its early days, but only Johnson and Christy Mathewson were part of the original Hall of Fame class of five players elected in 1936. The Big Train died in 1946.

Jones, Chipper

Chipper Jones is a third baseman for the Atlanta Braves. Born Larry Jones in Florida in 1972, Jones got the nickname Chipper because he was considered a "chip-off-the-old-block" of his father, also named Larry. Chipper was the first overall pick in the 1990 amateur draft. He joined the Braves in 1993, and in 1995, he helped the club with its first and only World Series title since moving to Atlanta in 1966. He was named N.L. MVP in 1999 and won the first of his two Silver Slugger Awards.

He has played in six All-Star Games in his career, and made the playoffs in his first 11 seasons in the Major Leagues. In the regular season, Jones is a lifetime .310 hitter with nine seasons of at least 100 RBI and six seasons of at least 30 home runs. In 2008, he became just the third switch-hitter in baseball history to reach the 400 home-run level. He also won his first batting title with a career-best .364 mark.

Joss, Addie

Joss was a right-handed pitcher in the Major Leagues with the Cleveland Indians from 1902–1910. Despite pitching only nine seasons, Joss put together a Hall-of-Fame career. He posted four straight 20-win seasons from 1905 through 1908, and his 1.89 ERA remains the second best in baseball history. He pitched a perfect game in 1908 in the heat of a pennant race. Late in the 1910 season, he became ill with meningitis, a serious brain disease, which eventually caused his death in 1911 at the age of only 31. His fellow players held a special game in his honor to raise money for his family. Joss was elected to the Hall of Fame in 1978.

Jump, Get a

The phrase "get a jump" means to get a quick running start, either on the bases when trying to advance from one base to another, such as on a stolen-base attempt, or in the field when trying to track down a ball. It does not mean that the player actually jumps in the air.

Junkballer

A junkballer is a pitcher who does not have a very good fastball but instead relies on a variety of breaking balls (curveballs, sliders, etc.) and other off-speed pitches (such as changeups), or unusual pitches (like a high-arcing Eephus pitch) to get batters out.

■ *Outfielder David Dellucci got a good jump on this ball and dove to make the catch.*

■ *Kaline was only 20 when he won a batting title.*

Kaline, Al

The man who would come to be known as Mr. Tiger was just a boy when he made his debut with Detroit in 1953 at age 18. Two years later, Kaline became the youngest batting champion in history, when his .340 average topped the American League. He played 20 seasons, batting .300 or better nine times and finishing with 3,007 hits. He finished among the top 10 in the A.L. MVP balloting nine times. Kaline made 15 All-Star teams, won 10 A.L. Gold Glove Awards and helped the Tigers to the 1968 World Series title. That year, he batted .379 in a seven-game triumph over the St. Louis Cardinals. He was elected to the Hall of Fame in 1980.

Kansas City Athletics

After playing in Philadelphia from 1901–1954, the A's left the city of Brotherly Love and moved to Kansas City for the 1955 season. The team remained near the bottom of the American League standings throughout its tenure in Missouri, finishing last or next-to-last 10 times in 13 years. After the 1967 season, the A's moved to Oakland, where they have remained ever since.

Kansas City Royals

Please see pages 14–15.

Keefe, Tim

One of the game's best pitchers before the turn of the 20th century, Keefe won 342 games with the four teams from 1880–1893. A submarine-style pitcher, the right-hander also played at a time when the pitching mound was just 50 feet from home plate, making him that much more difficult to hit. He won 40 games in a season twice, 30 games six times, and 20 games seven times. He was elected to the Hall of Fame in 1964.

Keeler, Willie

"Wee Willie" stood just 5 feet 7 inches (1.5 m), but he was a giant with the bat. He coined the phrase, "Hit 'em where they ain't" to describe the best way to achieve success at the plate. That advice may have sounded simple because Keeler made hitting look simple. He posted 15 straight seasons of .300 or better, topped by a .432 mark in 1897. That year, he set a record with a 44-game hitting streak. It lasted until 1941, when it was broken by Joe DiMaggio. Keeler retired with a .341 lifetime average, and when he went into the Hall of Fame in 1939, his plaque called him the "greatest place-hitter" and "best bunter" in baseball history.

Keeping Score

This is the term for tracking all of the play-by-play at a baseball game. Sportswriters and other members of the media keep score to help them with their reports after the game. Many fans like to keep score to help them follow the action or to remember the game years later.

Players on the field are numbered 1 through 9 (see box). Thus, a fly ball caught by the right fielder is scored "9." A double-play ground ball fielded by the shortstop,

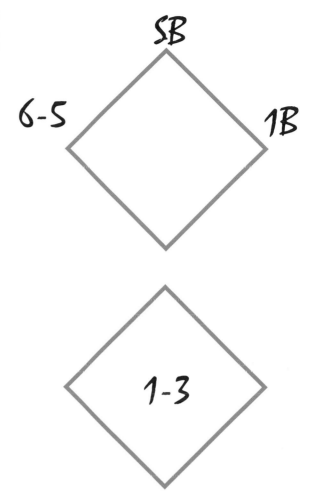

■ *The top batter got a single, stole second, and was thrown out at third by the shortstop. The bottom batter grounded out, pitcher to first.*

thrown to the second baseman, and then to the first baseman is scored "6-4-3." Strikeouts are scored with a K and called strikeouts get a backward K. Other plays in a game get their own symbols, such as BB for a base on balls (also called a walk), or E for an error. People can create their own unique scoring system for tracking batters' trips around the bases, but most systems use some form of these notations.

POSITION NUMBERS FOR KEEPING SCORE

PITCHER: **1**	THIRD BASEMAN: **5**
CATCHER: **2**	SHORTSTOP: **6**
FIRST BASEMAN: **3**	LEFT FIELDER: **7**
SECOND BASEMAN: **4**	CENTER FIELDER: **8**
RIGHT FIELDER: **9**	

Kansas City Royals

The Athletics left Kansas City for Oakland in 1967, but the town had proven that it was big-league quality. When the American League expanded in 1969, Kansas City was given a new team, which was named the Royals. The Royals quickly grew into a contender, and by 1976 they had won the first of three consecutive American League West titles.

In each of those three years, however, the Royals lost the American League Championship Series to the New York Yankees. In 1976, the Royals were beaten in the decisive fifth game by a Chris Chambliss home run, in 1977 they blew a two-run lead in the ninth inning of Game Five, and in 1978 they lost to the Yankees in four games.

But in 1980, the Royals finally broke through. Third baseman George Brett, who hit .390 that season, led them back to the

■ *World champs! The Royals celebrate their victory over the Cardinals in the 1985 Fall Classic.*

playoffs against the Yankees—and, this time, past them. Brett's upper-deck home run off New York's Goose Gossage in Game Three at Yankees Stadium clinched the sweep. The Philadelphia Phillies beat the Royals in six games in the World Series.

The Royals also lost in the playoffs in 1981 and 1984, but one of their most famous moments came in 1983, again against the Yankees. Brett homered off Gossage in the ninth inning at Yankee Stadium to give the Royals a 5–4 lead of a game on July 18. New York manager Billy Martin protested, though, claiming Brett had too much pine tar on his bat. The umpires agreed, and overturned the home run, giving the Yankees the win. After a lengthy protest, the A.L. president restored the home run and ordered that the game be continued with the Royals ahead. (They went on to win.)

In 1985, Kansas City finally broke through and won the first World Series in its history. Facing their Missouri rivals, the St. Louis Cardinals, in the "I-70 World Series" (named for a major highway that connected the two cities), the Royals trailed three games to two entering Game Six. Down one

run in the ninth, the Royals benefited from an incorrect call at first base that ignited a game-winning rally. The next night, the Royals won 11–0 to earn the championship.

Though the Royals have not been back to the postseason since, they have developed some big stars. Brett went onto the Hall of Fame, pitcher Bret Saberhagen won two Cy Young Awards, and Bo Jackson became the biggest star in sports in the late 1980s as an All-Star outfielder for the Royals and an all-pro running back with the NFL's Los Angeles Raiders.

The growing economic split in the Major Leagues between big and small cities hit the Royals hard, as they were no longer able to sign young stars (like outfielders Jermaine Dye, Carlos Beltran, and Johnny Damon) to big contracts. Stuck in an almost constant state of rebuilding, the Royals have had just one winning season since 1993.

■ *Mark Teahen takes a big rip.*

KANSAS CITY ROYALS

LEAGUE: **AMERICAN**

DIVISION: **CENTRAL**

YEAR FOUNDED: **1969**

CURRENT COLORS:
ROYAL BLUE AND WHITE

STADIUM (CAPACITY):
KAUFFMAN STADIUM (38,030)

ALL-TIME RECORD
(THROUGH 2008):
3,078–3,263

WORLD SERIES TITLES
(MOST RECENT): **1 (1985)**

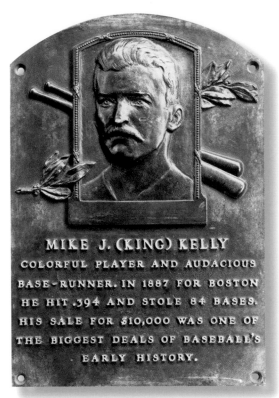

This is King Kelly's Hall-of-Fame plaque.

Kelly, Michael "King"

Kelly was one of the first stars of baseball's early days. He helped modernize the game by making popular the hit-and-run and the hook slide. He also helped change the rules. During one game, he was sitting on the bench when a foul ball was hit near his dugout. Kelly called out "Kelly now catching! Kelly now catching!" to the umpire and caught the ball for the out. A rule was then instituted that substitutions could only be made between plays, not during plays!

Kelly debuted in 1878 with the Cincinnati Reds, and then moved on to help the Chicago White Stockings win five N.L.

pennants between 1880 and 1886. Kelly won two batting titles along the way.

Kelly was a daring baserunner who helped make the hook slide an important part of the game. He was so adept at it that the phrase, "Slide, Kelly, slide!" entered the baseball language and became a popular song.

After the 1886 season, Kelly was sold to Boston for a then-record $10,000, a staggering sum at the time for a single player. He later played and managed in the Player's Association for a Cincinnati team named Kelly's Killers.

Kelly retired in 1893 with a .308 lifetime average. He died in 1894 and was inducted into the Hall of Fame in 1945.

Kent, Jeff

Dodgers second baseman Jeff Kent is one of the top run-producing middle infielders ever. (A middle infielder is a second baseman or shortstop; the players at those positions are usually known mostly for their defense.) In 2005, Kent became the first man to hit 300 career home runs as a second baseman. He entered 2009 with 377 home runs and 1,518 RBI in 17 seasons. A five-time All-Star, Kent debuted with the Toronto Blue Jays in 1992, but his best seasons came with San Francisco. In 2000, he batted a career-best .334 with 33 home runs and 125 RBI for the Giants to earn N.L. MVP honors.

Killebrew, Harmon

Few players had the raw power of Harmon Killebrew, a slugger who smashed 573 homers with the Washington Senators, Minnesota Twins, and Kansas City Royals from 1954 through 1975. Killebrew retired as the second-most prolific home run hitter in American League history (behind only Babe Ruth) and the greatest right-handed home-run hitter of all-time (since passed by Frank Robinson, Willie Mays, Hank Aaron, and Sammy Sosa).

Killebrew was born in Idaho and made his Major-League debut at age 17 in 1954. Over his first five seasons, some of which was spent in the minor leagues, Killebrew played just 113 games and struck out 93 times. But after becoming a starter in 1959, he had 42 home runs, the first of eight 40-homer seasons. He also drove in 105 runs, which marked his first of nine 100-RBI seasons.

Killebrew's massive power numbers earned him the nickname "Killer," though he was actually a very gentle and quiet man. The Senators moved to Minnesota to become the Twins for the 1961 season, but Killebrew kept right on slugging, hitting at least 40 homers in each of his first four seasons in Minnesota. In 1965, he led the Twins to their first American League pennant, and in 1969 he was named the American League MVP as the Twins won the A.L. West.

Killebrew played for the Royals in 1975 and then retired. He was elected to the Hall of Fame in 1984.

Kiner, Ralph

Kiner was one of baseball's greatest power hitters, but a back injury limited him to just 10 seasons. He later gained fame as a broadcaster with the Mets.

■ *Killebrew was one of baseball's top sluggers of the 1960s.*

two short of the National League record. Kiner made six consecutive All-Star teams from 1948–1953, but he was traded to the Cubs in the middle of the 1953 season. He retired after the 1955 season with 369 home runs in just 10 years of play. In 1962, he joined the expansion New York Mets as an announcer, and he hosted a postgame interview show known as *Kiner's Korner*. He was elected to the Hall of Fame as a player in 1975.

Klein, Chuck

A force at the plate, on the basepaths, and in the field, Klein was a Hall-of-Fame outfielder in the 1920s and '30s, mostly with the Philadelphia Phillies. He was named the 1932 N.L. MVP, and he led the league in home runs four times and in RBIs three times. He also won a batting title and a stolen-base title. In 1930, he set a big-league record for right fielders with 44 outfield assists, and in 1933 he won the Triple Crown by batting .368 with 28 home runs and 120 RBI. In 1936, he hit four home runs in a single game. He retired in 1939 and was elected to the Hall of Fame in 1980.

Klem, Bill

Arguably the best umpire in baseball history, Klem served in the National League from 1905 to 1941, almost entirely as a home-plate umpire, where he originat-

■ *Klein is one of baseball's least-known sluggers.*

He debuted with the Pittsburgh Pirates in 1946, and in 1947 hit 51 home runs, the first of two seasons over 50. His huge blasts into the left-field stands at Forbes Field in Pittsburgh led many to call the area Kiner's Korner. In 1949, Kiner hit 54 home runs,

ed the use of arm signals for calling balls and strikes. He was nicknamed "The Old Arbitrator" and umpired 18 World Series.

Knickerbocker Baseball Club

The New York Knickerbockers are often considered the first organized team in baseball history, and played the game under rules that would be recognizable to fans of the modern game. The team was founded by Hall of Famer Alexander Cartwright, who—with fellow club members that included Daniel Adams—developed most of the rules of the modern game. The team actually played at the Elysian Fields in Hoboken, New Jersey, across the Hudson River from Manhattan. Cartwright established 20 rules for his new club, among them noting "that the ball be pitched, not thrown." The club's first official game was played on June 18, 1846, on the Elysian Fields. Surprisingly, the team lost 23–1 to a rival New York club.

Knob

The knob of a bat is the rounded part at the very bottom of a bat. Most hitters hold the bat with their bottom hand resting on top of the knob. If a hitter holds his hands above the knob, he is said to be "choking up" on the bat. A few batters even wrap their bottom pinky finger below the knob of the bat. The knob is also used to help choose sides for pickup games. One

team's captain holds the bat near the barrel, and the other puts his hand above the first player's hand, and they continue trading off until one reaches the knob.

Knuckleball

The knuckleball is a pitch that is thrown with the fingernails, not the knuckles. It has very little spin, which makes it move unpredictably—and thus is difficult to hit, as well as to catch. Hall-of-Famers Hoyt Wilhelm and Phil Niekro threw the knuckleball, as well as Joe Niekro, Tom Candiotti, and, most recently, Tim Wakefield. The ball is gripped by digging the fingernails into the ball and keeping the palm off the ball. It is then thrown with a sort of pushing motion.

■ *This is the grip used to throw a knuckleball.*

Koufax, Sandy

Considered by some to be the greatest pitcher of all time, Sandy Koufax was a left-handed starter with the Brooklyn and Los Angeles Dodgers from 1955 through 1966. Though he struggled with his control at the start of his career, he eventually developed into a nearly unhittable pitcher who won the Cy Young Award in 1963, 1965, and 1966 before being forced to retire at age 30 because of arthritis in his left elbow.

■ *Koufax was the first to throw four no-hitters; he is shown here after No. 4 in 1965.*

Koufax was born and raised in Brooklyn, but he attended the University of Cincinnati on a basketball scholarship. In 1954, he played baseball for the Bearcats and attracted the attention of a Dodgers' scout who signed him.

Koufax debuted with his hometown Brooklyn Dodgers in 1955 (the Dodgers did not move to Los Angeles until the 1958 season). For his first six seasons, though, he was a very pedestrian pitcher, with just a 36–40 record. But in 1961, he showed signs of promise for the first time, going 18–13 with a 3.52 ERA and setting a National League record by striking out 269 batters.

Beginning in 1962, Koufax embarked on a five-year stretch that is among the best in baseball history. In 1962, he pitched his first no-hitter, the first of four consecutive years he would pitch a no-no, and he won the first of five straight N.L. ERA titles. In 1963, he won the pitching Triple Crown—leading the league in wins, strikeouts, and ERA—was named N.L. MVP, and led the Dodgers to the World Series title, where he captured MVP honors. He also topped 300 strikeouts (306) for the first time.

In 1964, Koufax won 19 games, and in 1965, he won his second Cy Young Award and pitched a perfect game. That same year, he set a new National League record and, at the time, Major-League record with 382

strikeouts. He led the Dodgers to another World Series title and again captured Series MVP honors. He also earned great acclaim for staying true to his Jewish heritage and refusing to pitch in a World Series game that fell on the Jewish holiday of Yom Kippur.

■ *Koufax: still a Dodgers' legend.*

In 1966, he won 27 games with a 1.73 ERA and helped the Dodgers to another pennant, though they lost the Series to the Baltimore Orioles.

After the Series, Koufax was forced to retire because of consistent pain and debilitating arthritis in his pitching arm. He retired with a 165–87 record, a lifetime ERA of 2.76, and 2,396 strikeouts. All three Cy Young Awards he won were unanimous, and all came in an era when only one pitcher in the sport was given the award each year.

For his career, Koufax struck out more than one batter per inning (2,396 strikeouts in 2,324.1 innings). His rate of 9.28 strikeouts for every nine innings pitched ranks fifth in big-league history.

In 1972, Koufax was elected to the Hall of Fame. At age 36, he was the youngest man ever enshrined in Cooperstown.

.426, an American League record that has never been topped.

After that amazing season, the Phillies tried to force Lajoie to play for them by getting a court order that said the only team in Pennsylvania he could play for was the Phillies. To solve the problem, Lajoie was sent to the Cleveland Indians. Lajoie was so popular that the team was known as the Naps while he played for them.

Lajoie stayed in Cleveland through the 1914 season, then returned to the Athletics and finished his career back in Philadelphia in 1915 and 1916. Overall, he batted .339, had 3,242 hits, and was arguably the American League's best second baseman of the dead-ball era. He was inducted into the Hall of Fame in 1937.

Landis, Kenesaw Mountain

Kenesaw Mountain Landis, a former United States District Court judge, was the first commissioner of baseball. He was best known for banning eight Chicago White Sox players, known as the "Black Sox," from the game for life for their supposed involvement in throwing (losing games on purpose) the 1919 World Series.

Though Landis was praised for his role in making baseball gain back the nation's respect by throwing those players out, he also deserves blame for keeping black players and other non-white players out of baseball during his time in charge. He re-

■ *White Sox superstar Napoleon Lajoie.*

Lajoie, Nap

Known for his graceful style in the field and a hard-hitting bat, Napoleon Lajoie (pronounced LAH-zho-way) was a top hitter in the early days of the American League. He began his career with the Philadelphia Phillies in the National League in 1896, but jumped to the upstart Athletics across town for the American League's debut season in 1901. That year, he batted

mained as commissioner until his death in 1944, and was elected to the Hall of Fame the same year.

Lasorda, Tommy

Few men have brought more joy, passion, or attention to baseball than Tommy Lasorda, who was the Dodgers' manager from 1976 until 1996.

As a Major-League pitcher, Lasorda never amounted to much, going just 0–4 in 26 games spread over the 1954, 1955 (both with the Brooklyn Dodgers), and 1956 (with the Kansas City Athletics) seasons. After a few years as a scout, he was a manager in the Dodgers' minor-league system from 1966 until 1973, when he joined the big-league club as a coach. Just before the end of the 1976 season, Walter Alston retired as the Dodgers' manager, a position he had held since 1954. Lasorda replaced him, and stayed for 20 years, winning 1,599 games, eight National League West titles, four pennants, and two World Series championships.

Lasorda often says he "bleeds Dodger blue," and he encouraged his players with his childlike enthusiasm for the team and the game. He was voted into the Hall of Fame in 1997, and managed the U.S. Olympic team to the gold medal at the 2000 Summer Olympics.

Lazzeri, Tony

Hall-of-Famer Tony Lazzeri was the second baseman on the New York Yankees' famous 1927 team. That team, dubbed "Murderers' Row" for its power-laden lineup, is sometimes considered the greatest baseball team in history.

Lazzeri played 12 years for the Yankees (1926–1937; he also played for three teams in 1938–39). Though often overshadowed by Babe Ruth and Lou Gehrig, he drove in more than 100 runs seven times, and helped the Yankees win five World Series. In one game in 1936, he hit two grand slams and drove in a league-record 11 runs.

■ *The former Dodgers' manager remains a baseball ambassador.*

23

■ *Red Sox fans celebrated their team's win in the A.L.'s 2007 League Championship Series.*

League Championship Series

Also known as the LCS, this is the playoff series one round before the World Series. The last two remaining play-off teams from each league (the winners of the League Division Series) face each other in a best-of-seven contest to see who will win their league's pennant and advance to the World Series.

The LCS began in 1969, when baseball split its leagues into divisions, with both the American League and National League having an East and West division. The winners of those divisions faced off in the LCS.

From then through 1984 it was a best-of-five series. It became best-of-seven in 1985. Until the wild-card era began with the 1995 playoffs, the LCS was the only post-season round other than the World Series.

Left Field

This is the area of the diamond from the third base, or left-field foul line, all the way over toward center field. In scorekeeping, the left fielder is known by the number 7. Because it is a corner outfield spot, athletes who play there must have strong arms to throw the ball anywhere on the infield.s.

Lemon, Bob

Bob Lemon began his big-league career as a third baseman in 1941. Five years later, after Lemon served in the Navy during World War II, Indians manager Lou Boudreau turned him into a pitcher. Lemon didn't like the idea at first, but he went on to become one of the best right-handers ever. In 1948, just two seasons after switching to his new position, Lemon tossed a no-hitter, won 20 games, and earned an All-Star nod. He also notched a pair of victories over the Boston Braves in the World Series that year, including Cleveland's clinching win in Game Six. Lemon went on to win 207 games in just 13 seasons as a pitcher and was inducted into the Hall of Fame in 1976. In 1978, he managed the New York Yankees to a World Series title.

Line Drive

A line drive is a hard-hit ball that stays straight, as if on a line, as it moves. If a line drive is caught before it hits the ground, the batter is out.

Lineup

The lineup for a baseball team lists who will play, the order in which players will come to bat, and where they will play in the field. There are nine players in the lineup at all times. Once the game starts and a player is removed from the lineup, he cannot go back in.

Traditionally, lineups place the fastest players, and those most likely to get on base, in the first (called "leadoff") and second spots in the order. The team's best hitter usually bats third, the power hitters are fourth and fifth, and the worst hitters are eighth and ninth. In the National League, the pitcher almost always bats ninth.

Little League

Little League is the name of a baseball and softball league for children that is the most popular of its kind around

continued on page 30

■ *A Little Leaguer swings for the fences!*

Los Angeles Angels of Anaheim

The Los Angeles Angels were part of the first American League expansion in 60 years when they joined the league before the 1961 season. The team has undergone several name changes, from the Los Angeles Angels (1961–65) to the California Angels (1965–1996) to the Anaheim Angels (1997–2004) to the Los Angeles Angels of Anaheim (2005–present). The Angels have been one of the game's top teams in recent years, but they didn't start out that way. Initially, they were known best for being owned by Gene Autry, a former actor famous for playing singing cowboys in the movies. It wasn't until 1979 that the Angels finally reached the postseason, winning the American League West behind an MVP season from Don Baylor and the flame-throwing pitching of Nolan Ryan, who set a big-league record by striking out 383 batters in 1973.

Even though Ryan left after that 1979 season, the Angels remained a force, winning the A.L. West in both 1982 and 1986. Each season ended traumatically for their fans, however. In 1982, the Angels took a two-games-to-none lead in the best-of-five A.L. Championship Series against the Milwaukee Brewers, only to lose three straight games. In 1986, the Angels jumped out to a three-games-to-one lead on the Boston Red Sox in the ALCS, which by then was best-of-seven. In Game Five, the Angels took a 5–2 lead

■ *Hall-of-Famer Rod Carew played for the Angels from 1979–1985.*

into the top of the ninth and were three outs from their first pennant. But a pair of two-run home runs gave the Red Sox the lead, and, though the Angels tied the score in the bottom of the ninth, they lost in extra innings. They went on to lose Games Six and Seven in Boston to drop the series.

In 1995, it appeared the Angels would make it back to the playoffs, but they blew an 11-game lead in August and lost a playoff to the Seattle Mariners for the A.L. West crown.

In 1996, the franchise was taken over by the Disney Corporation. In 2002, the Angels finally had a team capable of reaching the playoffs again, and they did just that by earning the A.L.'s wild card spot. They steamrollered through the American League playoffs to reach their first World Series, where it seemed heartbreak awaited their fans once again. Trailing in the Series three-games-to-two and down 5–0 in the seventh inning of Game Six, manager Mike Scioscia's team rallied to win. Then the Angels took Game Seven the next night to win their first World Series

■ *Outfielder Vladimir Guerrero is a hitting machine.*

championship. The Angels' comebacks popularized an odd mascot called the Rally Monkey, which began as a video clip of a monkey jumping up and down.

In 2004, the Angels signed star outfielder Vladimir Guerrero to a big free-agent contract. He hit .337 with 39 homers to earn league MVP honors that year. He also led the Angels to the first of five division titles in six years.

In 2008, the team had baseball's best record (100–62) and won a division title. Guerrero matched Lou Gehrig with his 13th season of 25 HRs and .300 average.

LOS ANGELES ANGELS OF ANAHEIM

LEAGUE: **AMERICAN**

DIVISION: **WEST**

YEAR FOUNDED: **1961**

CURRENT COLORS: **RED AND WHITE**

STADIUM (CAPACITY): **ANGEL STADIUM (45,050)**

ALL-TIME RECORD (THROUGH 2008): **3,790–3,856**

WORLD SERIES TITLES (MOST RECENT): **1 (2002)**

Los Angeles Dodgers

The Dodgers moved to Los Angeles before the 1958 season, leaving behind broken-hearted fans in Brooklyn but thrilling Los Angeles fans who had waited many years for a Major-League team. Unlike the Brooklyn Dodgers, who took decades to win the team's first World Series, the Los Angeles Dodgers took just two seasons to win one, doing so in 1959.

■ *Duke Snider was the "Duke of Flatbush."*

At the time, the Dodgers played in the massive Los Angeles Memorial Coliseum, and they drew crowds of more than 90,000 for their World Series games. In 1962, the team moved into new Dodger Stadium, where they remain to this day.

When the Dodgers first moved to California, they were led by offensive stars such as Duke Snider and Gil Hodges, but by the early 1960s they had evolved into a team led by a dominant pitching staff. Hall-of-Famers Sandy Koufax and Don Drysdale combined to win four Cy Young awards in the five years from 1962 through 1966, with three of them by Koufax. Those two keyed the Dodgers to World Series titles in 1963 (a sweep of the New York Yankees) and 1965 (a seven-game triumph over the Minnesota Twins), and to the N.L. pennant in 1966 (they lost the Series to the Baltimore Orioles).

Arm trouble forced Koufax into early retirement after the 1966 season, and the team dropped steadily from contention and was forced to rebuild. By 1974, however, the Dodgers were ready to contend again. They won the N.L. pennant, the last by long-time manager Walter Alston. The core of the team was the infield, featuring Steve Garvey at first base, Davey Lopes at second, Bill Russell at shortstop, and Ron Cey at third base. The Dodgers, now led by fiery manager Tommy Lasorda, again won N.L. pennants in 1977 and 1978, but lost the World Series both years to the New York Yankees.

The Dodgers made it back to the Fall Classic in 1981. That team was led by Cy Young winner and Rookie of the Year Fernando Valenzuela. The left-hander inspired "Fernandomania" in Los Angeles with his stellar pitching, unusual windup, and Mexican heritage.

In the World Series that year, the Dodgers trailed the Yankees two games to none before rallying to win four consecutive games for their first championship in 16 years.

In 1988, led by Cy Young winner Orel Hershiser and MVP Kirk Gibson, Los Angeles again won the N.L. West. After shocking the Mets in the NLCS, the Dodgers pulled an even bigger upset by beating the powerhouse Oakland A's in five games in the World Series. That Series is remembered most for Gibson's famous home run. The Dodgers were losing 4–3 in the bottom of the ninth inning of Game One. Gibson, who was injured in both legs and thought to be too hurt to play in the Series, came off the bench to pinch-hit against Oakland's Dennis Eckersley. After working the count to three balls and two strikes, Gibson hit a one-armed home run to win the game, then limped around the bases.

The Dodgers haven't won the World Series since, although they have featured great players such as catcher Mike Piazza and Japanese pitcher Hideo Nomo.

The team remains incredibly popular in Los Angeles, where it regularly draws more than 3 million fans each season. In 2008, the Dodgers hired Joe Torre, the former manager of the New York Yankees, to be their new skipper in hopes he could do what he did four times in the Bronx: win the World Series.

■ *Russell Martin is L.A.'s star catcher.*

LOS ANGELES DODGERS

LEAGUE: **NATIONAL**

DIVISION: **WEST**

YEAR FOUNDED: **1884**

CURRENT COLORS: **BLUE AND WHITE**

STADIUM (CAPACITY): **DODGER STADIUM (56,000)**

ALL-TIME RECORD (THROUGH 2008): **9,960–9,050**

WORLD SERIES TITLES (MOST RECENT): **6 (1988)**

■ *Lofton was a smart and speedy baserunner.*

Location

Location is one of the most important aspects of pitching. It refers to where a ball is pitched. The best pitchers are able to vary their location so that they can throw strikes without throwing the ball where it can be hit easily and hard by the batter.

Lofton, Kenny

Kenny Lofton first gained attention in the sports world not as a baseball player but as the backup point guard on the 1988 Arizona Wildcats basketball team that advanced to the NCAA Final Four. He debuted in the Major Leagues in 1991 with the Houston Astros, and the next season joined the Cleveland Indians, with whom he spent the majority of his career. He played in the first of six consecutive All-Star Games in 1994, and in 1995 he helped the Indians to the World Series for the first time in 41 years.

One of the fastest players in the game, Lofton stole 54 or more bases five straight seasons beginning in 1992, including 75 in 1996. For his career, he stole 622 bases, placing him 15th in Major-League history. After a one-year stint with the Atlanta Braves in 1997, Lofton returned to Cleveland and stayed with the Indians through the 2001 season. After that, however, he began bouncing around the big leagues, playing with eight different teams over the next six seasons before finally going to the

the country. It was founded in 1939 and now includes six divisions, ranging in ages from 5 through 18. Its most famous element is the Little League World Series, held annually in Williamsport, Pennsylvania, where Little League was founded. The Little League World Series is a tournament featuring teams made up of kids ages 10 through 12 from around the world. The final matches the winner of the eight-team U.S. bracket against the winner of an eight-team bracket of international teams.

Indians for a third time to finish the 2007 season. Lofton is eligible for Hall-of-Fame consideration beginning in 2013.

Los Angeles Angels of Anaheim

Please see pages 26–27.

Los Angeles Dodgers

Please see pages 28–29.

Losing Streaks

A losing streak occurs any time a team or a pitcher loses more than one game in a row. The 1961 Philadelphia Phillies set a big-league record by losing 23 straight games. In 1988, the Baltimore Orioles lost 21 straight games to start the season. Pitcher Anthony Young of the New York Mets set a record by dropping 27 straight decisions from 1992 to 1993.

Louisville Slugger®

The Louisville Slugger® is a model of baseball bat made by the Hillerich & Bradsby Company in Louisville, Kentucky. The first bat was made in 1884 by Bud Hillerich. He supposedly made one for Pete Browning, a hitting star at the time for Louisville's National League team. The batmakers at Hillerich & Bradsby also popularized the concept of putting a player's name on the bat. Hillerich & Bradsby remains the most famous bat maker in the country today, having been used by players such as Babe Ruth, Hank Aaron, Ted Williams, and Derek Jeter.

Lyons, Ted

Ted Lyons pitched 21 seasons in the Major Leagues: from 1923 through 1942, and then five games in 1946. He won 260 games in his career while pitching entirely for the Chicago White Sox, who never won a pennant while he was there. A left-hander, Lyons led the American League in wins twice and ERA once, and had three 20-win seasons.

Late in his career, Lyons was limited almost entirely to pitching home games in Chicago on Sundays, and in 1942 he was effective enough at it to make 20 starts, completing them all, and winning the A.L. ERA crown at 2.10. He was elected to the Hall of Fame in 1955, and his plaque notes that he pitched both a no-hitter and a 21-inning game during his stellar career.

■ *The Louisville Slugger® is the bat of choice for many Major Leaguers, past and present.*

Mack, Connie

Cornelius Alexander "Connie" Mack is the winningest manager in Major League Baseball history—and it's not even close. In 53 seasons, with the last 50 coming for the Philadelphia Athletics beginning in 1901, "The Tall Tactician" won 3,731 games. That's nearly 1,000 more games than runner-up John McGraw (2,763).

Mack was a big-league catcher who took over as the player-manager of the National League's Pirates late in his playing career in 1894. He managed in Pittsburgh through the 1896 season, then became the Athletics' first manager when that team was part of the first year of the new American League in 1901.

For the next half century, Mack ruled the Athletics' dugout in his familiar business suit, with a rolled-up scorecard in his hand. In the early years of the new league, his teams won a pair of A.L. pennants. In 1910, Philadelphia won the World Series for the first of three times in four seasons. The Athletics also won back-to-back World Series in 1929 and 1930.

Mack was inducted into the National Baseball Hall of Fame in 1937.

■ *The manager known as "Mr. Mack."*

Maddux, Greg

Starting pitcher Greg Maddux is a four-time Cy Young Award winner who in 2004 became the 22nd big-leaguer to win 300 games in his career.

Maddux made his debut as a 20-year-old for the Chicago Cubs in 1986. He was a two-time All-Star in Chicago, with his best season coming in 1992. He won 20 games for the first time, compiled an ERA of 2.18, and was named the N.L.'s top pitcher.

Maddux parlayed that season into a big free-agent contract with the Atlanta Braves for 1993, and he did not disappoint his new club. He went on to win three more Cy Young Awards in a row while helping the Braves become the N.L.'s dominant team. In 11 seasons in Atlanta, Maddux earned six All-Star selections and led the league in ERA four times (twice with a

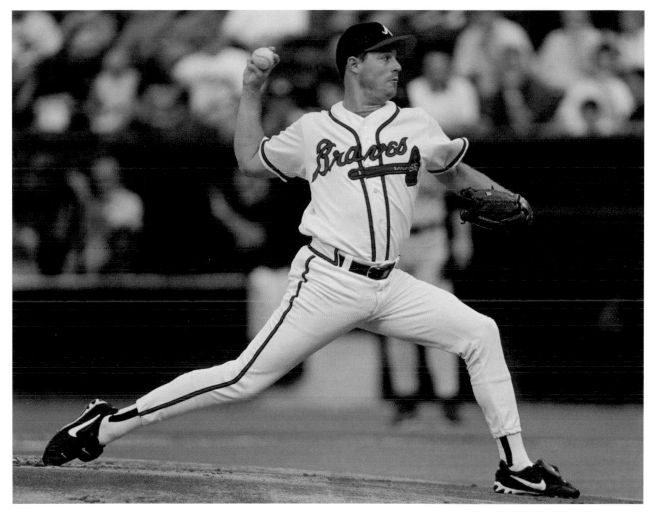

■ *Maddux had his greatest success with Atlanta, for whom he won three Cy Young Awards.*

mark below 2.00). He began his 23rd big-league season in 2008 as a member of the San Diego Padres and ended it with his second stint with the Dodgers.

Although Maddux fanned as many as 204 batters in a season (1998), he has not been known as a strikeout pitcher. Instead, he has relied on an assortment of pitches and pinpoint control. In 1997, for instance, he had almost as many victories (19) as he had walks (20).

The younger brother of former big-league pitcher Mike Maddux, Greg also is one of the best fielding pitchers ever. In 1990, he earned the N.L.'s Gold Glove Award for his position. That was his first of 17 Gold Gloves over 18 seasons.

Major League Baseball

Major League Baseball (MLB) is the governing body that organizes and operates the American League and

■ *MLB game action between Cincinnati and Boston.*

the National League. They are the only two recognized Major Leagues in baseball today, although other leagues historically have been listed as "Major."

Sixteen teams play in the National League (sometimes called the "Senior Circuit" because it is older), which first began play in 1876; 14 teams play in the American League (the "Junior Circuit"), which first began play in 1901.

Each of these two leagues is grouped into three divisions (East, Central, and West). The three division winners, plus the non-division winner with the best record in each league, advance to the playoffs. The four playoff teams in each league meet in

a pair of best-of-five Division Series. The two surviving teams then meet in a best-of-seven Championship Series to determine their league's pennant winner. The two pennant winners square off in the World Series, which is another best-of-seven, to determine baseball's champion.

The modern World Series, also known as the "Fall Classic," is one of the most famous sporting events in the world. It was first played in 1903, when the two leagues agreed to have their champions meet to determine a single champion of baseball. In 1904, the National League-champion New York Giants refused to play the winner of the fledgling American League, but the Series resumed in 1905. It was played every year after that until 1994, when a players' strike ended the regular season in August and wiped out the postseason. The Series resumed in 1995.

MLB's structure has changed over the years. Until 1969, each league operated as a single eight- or 10-team league. When both leagues expanded to 12 teams in 1969, the leagues were split into two six-team divisions for the first time. Further expansions resulted in the creation of a third division in each league.

MLB also has expanded its reach outside of the United States. In 1969, it placed a team in Canada for the first time when the Montreal Expos started. The Expos since have moved to Washington, D.C., but the Toronto Blue Jays were a second Canadian team added in 1977. The 1992 and '93 Blue Jays are the only Canadian teams to win the World Series.

More recently, MLB has expanded its reach with regular international telecasts and highlight shows. The league itself has taken on a more international flavor with an influx of talent from Latin America and Asia. MLB also has played several regular-season games overseas, most recently when the Boston Red Sox opened the 2008 season with a pair of games against the Oakland Athletics in Tokyo, Japan.

MLB also organizes the sale of thousands of souvenir items, produces the league Web site and TV contracts, and hircs and trains all umpires.

Manager

A manager is in charge of all on-field decisions for a baseball team. He is assisted by several coaches to whom he has assigned specific jobs. The manager usually decides who plays what position, where each player bats in the lineup, and when to remove a pitcher from the game. He also makes strategic in-game decisions from the dugout, such as when to bunt, steal, or hit-and-run. The manager signals those decisions to his base coaches, who then relay them to the batter or baserunners.

Hall-of-Famer manager Connie Mack won more games (3,731) and managed more seasons (53) than anyone else in Major League Baseball history.

Manley, Effa

Effa Manley was the co-owner and business manager of the Negro Leagues' Newark Eagles from 1936 to 1948. The Eagles won the Negro League

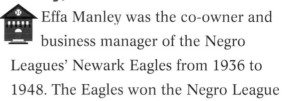

■ *Managers and umps sometimes disagree.*

■ *Mantle was another in a long line of Yankee greats.*

Mantle, Mickey

A switch-hitter who boasted a rare combination of power and speed, New York Yankees outfielder Mickey Mantle remains one of the most popular superstars in baseball history, even though his last game was more than 40 years ago.

Mantle played for 18 seasons beginning in 1951, when he was a rookie for the Yankees' World Series champs. He suffered a serious knee injury in the outfield during Game Two of the Fall Classic against the New York Giants that year. The injury robbed him of much of his speed and troubled him throughout the rest of his career. Still, he managed to belt 536 career home runs—not counting a record 18 in World Series play—while stealing 153 bases and batting .298 lifetime. His best overall season was 1956, when he batted .353 with 52 home runs and 130 RBI to win the A.L. Triple Crown. He also earned the first of his three league MVP awards that year (he finished in the top five another half-dozen times). Mickey helped the Yankees to 12 pennants and seven World Series championships.

Although some New York fans didn't warm to Mantle at first simply because he was not Joe DiMaggio—who played before him in center field in Yankee Stadium—most soon included his name among the list of Yankees' greats that also included the likes of Babe Ruth, Lou Gehrig, and Yogi Berra.

Mantle was elected to the Hall of Fame in 1969. He remained a fan favorite, and many people were sad when, after suffering from liver problems late in his life, he died in 1995.

World Series in 1946 and often were a top-division team, but it was for her skills at running the organization that Manley received notice.

Manley was known as an advocate for better conditions—including better salaries and better travel arrangements—for her players. And as an executive with the local chapter of the National Association for the Advancement of Colored People (NAACP), she often used Eagles' games to promote civic causes. Manley, who died at 81 in 1981, was inducted into the Baseball Hall of Fame in 2006. She was the first woman to be named to the Hall.

Marichal, Juan

A native of the Dominican Republic, Juan Marichal won 243 games in 16 Major-League seasons, most of them with the San Francisco Giants, from 1960 to 1975. In 1983, he became the first Latino pitcher inducted into the Hall of Fame.

The right-hander was known for his high leg kick during his windup and for his amazing control. That helped him win 20 or more games six times in his career, including a string of four seasons beginning in 1963. That year, he also hurled a no-hit game. Marichal's 26 wins in 1968 remain the most ever by a San Francisco pitcher.

Marichal, who was a nine-time All-Star, also was involved in one of baseball's ugliest incidents when he hit Dodgers catcher

Johnny Roseboro over the head with a baseball bat in a game in 1965. Marichal was suspended for eight days and fined. He always regretted the incident, and he and Roseboro eventually became friends.

Maris, Roger

Roger Maris was the Yankees' slugger who broke one of the most famous records in sports: Babe Ruth's 60 home runs in a single season. Maris hit 61 round-trippers in 1961 to topple Ruth's 34-year-old mark. Maris and teammate Mickey Mantle thrilled baseball fans that year as both men chased Ruth's record. Mantle tailed

■ *Maris broke a record that had stood for 34 years.*

off near the end of the season and finished with 54 home runs, while Maris belted his record breaker off Boston's Tracy Stallard on the final day of the season.

In all, Maris hit 275 homers in a 12-season career from 1957 to 1968. He was the A.L. MVP in both 1960 and '61. He hit 33 homers the year after his record-breaking season, but never topped 26 again.

Maris' single-season mark of 61 stood 37 years before it was bettered several times in the home-run boom of the late 1990s and early 2000s, first by Mark McGwire's 70 in 1998. Barry Bonds now holds the record of 73 home runs in 2001.

■ *Martinez was perhaps the best DH ever.*

Martinez, Edgar

Edgar Martinez could flat-out hit. In an 18-year career played exclusively with the Seattle Mariners from 1987 to 2004, "Papi" batted .312 with 309 home runs. He routinely hit better than .300, topped by American League-leading totals of .343 in 1992 and .356 in 1995.

Martinez began his career as a third baseman in a late-season call-up in 1987, but he was almost exclusively a designated hitter for the final decade of his big-league career. He was one of the best ever in that role, earning six of his seven All-Star nods after moving full-time to the DH. He drove in more than 100 runs six times in seven seasons beginning in 1995.

Mascots

Mascots are the costumed men and women who entertain fans with their antics on the field or in the stands during a baseball game. The San Diego Chicken and the Phillie Phanatic are two of the most commonly recognized mascots.

Mascots sometimes can be animals. For many years, the Philadelphia Athletics' mascot was an elephant because of a rude comment once made by New York Giants manager John McGraw. In the early days of baseball, too, uniformed kids who doubled as bat boys were the mascots for big-league teams. They were expected to bring their clubs good luck.

Mathewson, Christy

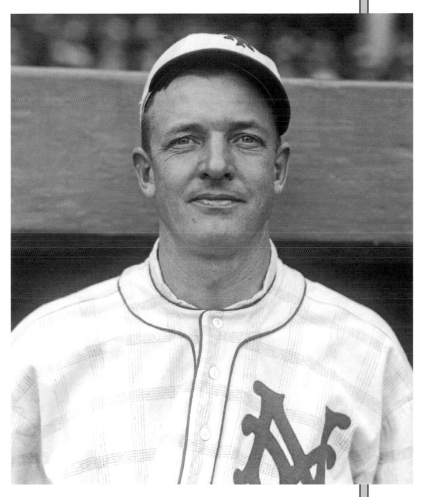

At the height of his career in the early 1900s, the New York Giants' Christy Mathewson was perhaps the most popular athlete in the United States. Eventually, he became one of the two pitchers among the National Baseball Hall of Fame's first-ever class of inductees in 1936.

In 17 seasons beginning in 1900 (with all but one appearance coming for the Giants), "Big Six" won 373 games—tied for third on baseball's all-time list—while compiling a sparkling ERA of 2.13. The right-hander won 20 or more games 13 times, and 30 or more games four times, including a 20th-century N.L. record of 37 victories in 1908. His most famous pitch was the "fadeaway," which broke in toward right-handed batters—the original screwball.

■ *Mathewson remains among baseball's all-time greats.*

Mathewson helped the Giants win four league pennants in his career. New York won only one World Series in that time, but in it, Mathewson put on the greatest pitching performance in the history of the Fall Classic. It came in 1905, when the Giants beat the Philadelphia Athletics in five games. Mathewson pitched complete-game shutouts in three of New York's four victories, includ-ing a four-hitter in the opener, a four-hitter in Game Three, and a six-hitter in the finale. He struck out 18 and walked only one.

Mathewson was just 45 when he died in 1925 from injuries suffered during World War I. He had been an officer in the Chemical Corps, and inhaled poisonous gases during a training exercise.

■ *Boston went all out to capture Dice-K from Japan.*

season in Milwaukee. He went on to man the hot corner almost every day for the Braves through their first season in Atlanta in 1966 before briefly playing for Houston and Detroit.

A right-handed thrower but a left-handed hitter, Mathews earned All-Star selections in nine different seasons and topped 30 home runs each year from 1953 to 1961. His 47 round-trippers in 1953 stood 27 years as the most by a third baseman. Mathews helped the 1957 and 1958 Braves to league pennants; the 1957 squad beat the Yankees in an exciting seven-game World Series.

Mathews, who grew up in Santa Barbara, California, earned a famous footnote by being featured on the cover of the first issue of *Sports Illustrated* magazine on August 16, 1954.

Mathews, Eddie

Eddie Mathews was the power-hitting third baseman for the Braves in three different cities in the 1950s and 1960s. He slugged 512 home runs in 17 big-league seasons in all from 1952 to 1968; at the time, he was one of only seven men to reach the 500 mark.

Mathews was a 20-year-old rookie who hit 25 home runs for the Boston Braves in 1952. The next year, he led the National League with 47 homers in the club's first

Mathewson, Christy

Please see page 39.

Matsuzaka, Daisuke

Daisuke Matsuzaka (DICE-kay mahtsoo-ZAHK-ah) is a Japanese-born starting pitcher for the Boston Red Sox. In his first season in the United States in 2007, he helped the Red Sox win their second World Series in four years.

"Dice-K," as he is known to his American fans, was a star in Japan's Pacific

League and MVP of the World Baseball Classic in 2006 before Boston won the bidding rights to sign him to a Major-League contract. In his first season in Boston, Matsuzaka went 15–12 and struck out 201 batters in 204.2 innings pitched during the regular season. He was the winning pitcher in the Red Sox' A.L. East-clinching victory over Minnesota late in September. He then won his lone start in Boston's four-game sweep of the Colorado Rockies in the World Series.

Matsuzaka is known for his wide assortment of pitches that includes a strong fastball to go along with various breaking balls and a changeup that often acts like a screwball. He got off to a blazing start in his second season with the Red Sox, and finished 2008 with an 18–3 record.

Mauer, Joe

The Minnesota Twins' Joe Mauer is one of the best-hitting catchers in baseball. In 2006, he hit .347 to become the first catcher ever to win an American League batting title, and the first ever to post the best average in the entire Major Leagues in a given season.

Mauer was just 18 when Minnesota made him the first pick of the amateur draft in 2001. He sailed through the Twins' farm system before beginning the 2004 season with the big-league club. Injuries limited him to only 107 at-bats that year, but he hit

.294 in 2005. Then came the breakout season in '06, when he drove in 84 runs to go along with his league-leading batting average. He earned his first All-Star berth that season and helped the Twins win the A.L. Central Division. Mauer won his second batting title with a .328 mark in 2008.

Mays, Willie

Please see page 42.

Mazeroski, Bill

Hall-of-Famer Bill Mazeroski was a 10-time All-Star and one of the finest fielding second basemen ever in a 17-year

■ *Mauer's sweet swing makes him a top-hitting catcher.*

Mays, Willie

Willie Mays' name inevitably comes up on the short list of greatest baseball players ever when that discussion rolls around. He excelled at all facets of the game—offensively, defensively, and on the bases—in 22 big-league seasons, mostly for the New York and San Francisco Giants.

■ *Mays got his "Say-Hey" nickname after his favorite greeting.*

Mays was the N.L. Rookie of the Year for the Giants' pennant-winning team in 1951. (Trivia note: He was on-deck when Bobby Thomson hit the famous "Shot Heard 'Round the World.") He missed most of the next two seasons while serving in the military, but was back in 1954 to earn an All-Star berth for the first of 19 years in a row and to earn the first of his two career MVP awards. He also helped the Giants win the World Series over the Cleveland Indians that year; his over-the-shoulder catch in Game One often is considered the finest defensive play in baseball history.

Mays, known as "The Say-Hey Kid," went on to hit 660 home runs in his career (he was only the second man, after Babe Ruth, to reach the 600 mark) while batting .302. His 1,903 career RBI still ranked in the all-time top 10 entering 2008, and he stole 338 bases in his career. The godfather of all-time home-run champ Barry Bonds, Mays also won 12 consecutive Gold Gloves beginning in 1957 for his play in center field.

career with Pittsburgh from 1956 to 1972. But he will forever be remembered for hitting one of the most dramatic home runs ever: the ninth-inning, tiebreaking blast in Game Seven of the 1960 World Series to lift the Pirates past the New York Yankees.

The Yankees had powered their way to three lopsided victories in the Series, while the underdog Pirates had scratched their way to three close wins. The final game was a back-and-forth affair that was tied at 9–9 when "Maz" stepped in against Ralph Terry to lead off the bottom of the ninth. Mazeroski took the first pitch for a ball; the second pitch he deposited over the fence in left field for the only walk-off home run ever in Game Seven of the World Series.

Mazeroski hit a modest .260 with 138 home runs in his career. On defense, though, he was an eight-time Gold Glove winner who was especially known for his ability to turn the double play.

McCarthy, Joe

Joe McCarthy managed the New York Yankees through a remarkable period of success from 1931 to 1946. His teams won eight A.L. pennants and seven World Series in that span, including four championships in a row beginning in 1936.

McCarthy never played big-league baseball, but he was a master at handling his players. Including managing for eight seasons with the Chicago Cubs (1926–1930)

■ *McCarthy guided his heroes to seven titles.*

and Boston Red Sox (1948–1950) before and after his stint with the Yankees, McCarthy posted a career record of 2,125 wins and 1,333 losses. His victory total stands eighth in Major-League history, and his winning percentage of .615 as a manager is the best ever.

In 24 seasons leading big-league ball clubs, McCarthy's teams never posted a losing record. Each of the teams he managed finished in the first division (a term that pre-dates modern baseball's division setup and means in the upper half of the league standings). He was inducted into the Hall of Fame in 1957.

■ *McCovey was known as "Willie Mac."*

McCovey, Willie

A gentle giant, Willie McCovey was soft-spoken off the field, but one of baseball's most feared sluggers of the 1960s and early 1970s on it. He is arguably the most beloved player in San Francisco baseball history.

McCovey's popularity with Giants' fans can be traced to the fact that he came up to the big club in San Francisco (other stars before him such as Willie Mays began their career in other cities). He had a pair of triples and a pair of singles in his big-league debut against future Hall-of-Famer Robin

Roberts in 1959. "Stretch" got his nickname for his long reach at first base, but he mostly played in the outfield until the Giants traded Orlando Cepeda in 1965.

The left-handed power hitter was a six-time All-Star who hit 521 home runs in his career, including an N.L.-record 18 grand slams. His best season came in 1969, when he batted .320 with 45 home runs and 126 RBI to earn league MVP honors.

He was traded to San Diego in what was thought to be the twilight of his career in 1974, and he also played briefly with the Oakland A's in 1976. But he returned to San Francisco as a free agent in 1977 and earned N.L. Comeback-Player-of-the-Year honors for belting 28 home runs at age 39.

McGraw, John

John McGraw was one of the best baseball players of the 1890s, but his real fame came as the iron-fisted manager of the New York Giants from 1902 to 1932. "Muggsy" won 2,763 games as a big-league manager, which ranks second all-time only behind Connie Mack.

McGraw got his managerial start while still playing for the N.L.'s Baltimore Orioles in 1899. He also managed the A.L.'s Baltimore Orioles (the team that became the New York Yankees) in 1901 and 1902 before taking over the Giants for the latter half of '02. In 29 full seasons as the Giants' manager, McGraw led his teams to a first- or second-place finish 21 times. The Giants won 10 pennants and three World Series on his watch, including back-to-back championships in 1921 and 1922.

McGraw was known for his tyrannical style and win-at-all-costs mentality (his other nickname was "The Little Napoleon" after the famous French emperor). But he also inspired fierce loyalty among his players and was one of the most innovative managers ever. He helped popularize strategies such as the hit-and-run and the squeeze play.

McGwire, Mark

Twelve-time All-Star Mark McGwire was one of the most imposing home-run hitters in baseball history. But after his retirement in 2001, he became mixed up in the steroids controversy that gripped Major League Baseball.

"Big Mac" was an effective pitcher in college at Southern California before Trojans coach Rod Dedeaux turned him into a full-time hitter. He soon became known for his mammoth home-run blasts, and the Oakland A's took him with the 10th pick

■ *A moment in history: Mark McGwire watches his record-tying 61st home run of 1998.*

in the 1984 draft. By 1987, he hit 49 home runs and was the A.L. Rookie of the Year.

After hitting 52 home runs for the A's in 1996, McGwire was traded to the St. Louis Cardinals midway through '97. In 1998, he and Sammy Sosa engaged in a home-run battle that thrilled the nation. Sosa finished with 66 round-trippers, but McGwire reached 70—a previously unthinkable level. (Barry Bonds eventually passed McGwire's mark with 73 homers in 2001.)

McGwire followed his record season with 65 homers in 1999 and ended his career in 2001 with 583 lifetime blasts in just 1,874 games. His rate of 1 home run for every 10.61 at-bats is the best in baseball history. But McGwire soon came under suspicion during the performance-enhanc-ing drug scandal. It is not known whether he took any such drugs, but in 2005, before a Congressional committee, he declined to answer questions under oath about steroid use in baseball. Two years later, he failed to gain induction into the Hall of Fame in his first year of eligibility.

Mendoza Line

The Mendoza Line is an imaginary batting-average line at the .200 level (.200 is a very poor mark). A player's whose average dips under .200 is said to have "fallen below the Mendoza Line."

Mario Mendoza was a notoriously light-hitting shortstop who batted .215 in nine big-league seasons with Pittsburgh, Seattle, and Texas from 1974 to 1982. Originally, .215 was used as the boundary for the Mendoza Line, but .200 has now become the standard.

Merkle's Mistake

Although he was an effective player for 16 big-league seasons, New York Giants infielder Fred Merkle is famous to this day for a disastrous base-running mistake that helped cost his team the pennant in 1908.

Here's what happened: The Giants and the Chicago

■ *Swings (and misses) like this one lead toward the Mendoza Line.*

Cubs were neck-and-neck in the battle for the N.L. pennant when they met at New York's Polo Grounds on September 23. With the score tied at 1–1 and two outs in the bottom of the ninth inning, Merkle singled, sending teammate Moose McCormick to third base. Al Bridwell followed with another single, apparently scoring McCormick. When Merkle saw McCormick cross home plate, he headed to the dugout before reaching second base. (In Merkle's defense, that was a common practice at the time.)

Chicago second baseman Johnny Evers, however, battled the crowd that had run onto the field to retrieve the baseball. He stepped on second base in view of the umpire, who declared Merkle out. Since Merkle never stepped on second, Evers actually "forced" Merkle out.

With fans overrunning the field, there was no way to continue the game. The Cubs argued for a forfeit; the Giants argued they had won. After considering statements from both sides—Chicago players said Merkle never touched second, while Giants' players said he had—N.L. President Harry Pulliam declared the game a tie. So when the teams ended the season tied atop the standings, "Merkle's Mistake" meant the game had to be replayed. Chicago won that repeat game 4–2 to clinch the pennant.

One footnote: In a recent book called *The Old Ball Game* (Grove/Atlantic, 2005), noted sports journalist Frank De-

■ *Unlucky—but talented—outfielder Fred Merkle.*

Ford asserts that Pulliam's decision turned on a letter by Christy Mathewson, the Giants' star pitcher. Mathewson, who was noted for his high level of honesty and sense of fair play, admitted that Merkle did not reach second base, but instead turned and headed to the dugout when he saw the winning run score.

Miller, Marvin

Marvin Miller is an important, though controversial, figure in baseball history. He is often praised—but also criticized—for helping build the Major League Baseball Players Association (MLBPA) into a powerful union during his 17 years as its executive director.

continued on page 52

■ *Slugging first baseman Prince Fielder leads the Brew Crew.*

Milwaukee Brewers

The best years of the current Milwaukee Brewers' franchise came in the early 1980s, when "Harvey's Wallbangers"—named for manager Harvey Kuenn, a former big-league player—pounded their way to the American League pennant and the club's lone World Series appearance. Milwaukee hadn't reached the playoffs until 2008, when they earned a National League wild-card berth with key victories on the final weekend of the season.

The Brewers began as an A.L. expansion team in 1969, but it wasn't in Milwaukee. The team was based in Seattle and was known as the Pilots. After just one season there, though, the team moved to Milwaukee and became the Brewers.

A string of losing seasons was brightened in 1974 by Robin Yount, an 18-year-old shortstop who would play his entire 20-year career in Milwaukee and go on to the Hall of Fame. Yount soon was joined in the lineup by big hitters such as Larry Hisle, Gorman Thomas, Cecil Cooper, and Ben Ogilvie, plus another future Hall of Famer in Paul Molitor, and in 1978 the Brewers posted their first winning season.

The team needed some pitching, though, to take the next step to the playoffs. So, in 1981, starter Pete Vuckovich and reliever Rollie Fingers arrived. Fingers, a veteran of the A's World Series teams in the 1970s, was spectacular his first year in Milwaukee. He won 6 games and saved 28, and had a sparkling ERA of 1.04. He was the first reliever ever to win the Cy Young and MVP awards in the same season.

More importantly, Milwaukee made the playoffs for the first time. Although the Brewers lost a dramatic seven-game series to the Yankees in the A.L. Championship Series, they were just getting warmed up. The next year, Yount was the league MVP, Vuckovich was the Cy Young Award winner, and Milwaukee caught fire after Kuenn took over as manager. The Brewers edged the Baltimore Orioles by one game to win the A.L. East. Then they downed the California Angels in five games in the A.L. Championship Series—Milwaukee won the last three games after dropping the first two—to advance to the World Series for the first time.

Although the World Series ended with a disappointing, seven-game loss to the St. Louis Cardinals, Brewers' fans figured another trip to the Fall Classic would be just around the corner. Unfortunately, it hasn't happened. Milwaukee has had some good players, such as two-time All-Star outfielder Greg Vaughn in the 1990s, but didn't make the postseason until 2008.

In 1998, the Brewers moved from the A.L. East to the newly formed N.L. Central. Three years later, the team was on the move again—this time out of County Stadium in Milwaukee into new Miller Park.

The Brewers began building a team that was similar to the old "Harvey's Wallbangers."

■ *Outfielder Ryan Braun.*

First, infielder Bill Hall came along to slug 35 home runs in 2006. Outfielder Corey Hart belted 24 homers and stole 23 bases the next year. And first baseman Prince Fielder (the son of former Major Leaguer Cecil Fielder) blasted a club-record 50 round-trippers in 2007.

Milwaukee was one of the surprise teams in baseball that year, winning 83 games. In 2008, the Brewers were even better. They won 90 games and clinched a wild-card berth on the final day of the season, even after replacing their manager late in September.

MILWAUKEE BREWERS

LEAGUE: **NATIONAL**

DIVISION: **CENTRAL**

YEAR FOUNDED: **1969**

CURRENT COLORS: **MIDNIGHT BLUE AND GOLD**

STADIUM (CAPACITY): **MILLER PARK (41,900)**

ALL-TIME RECORD (THROUGH 2008): **3,009–3,338**

WORLD SERIES TITLES: **NONE**

Minnesota Twins

Few franchises ever have experienced the ups and downs that the Minnesota Twins have gone through over the past couple of decades. The Twins have done it all in that span—from World Champions to also-rans to almost being extinct.

The history of the Twins' franchise actually began in Washington, D.C., in 1901.

■ *Oliva won three batting titles.*

The Washington Senators were a charter member of the American League's first season as a Major League.

In 60 years in Washington, the Senators never had much success. They won the World Series in 1924 and had one of the game's all-time great pitchers in Walter "Big Train" Johnson, but most of the time, the Senators wallowed in the bottom half of the league standings. Playing on a famous saying about George Washington, it was said that the Washington team was "first in war, first in peace, and last in the American League."

In 1961, interest in the Senators was at an all-time low. The club moved to the Twin Cities area of Minneapolis/St. Paul, Minnesota. That's how the team got its new name.

In their first season in Minnesota, the Twins weren't much better. But with Harmon Killebrew smashing home runs and Tony Oliva getting on base ahead of him, Minnesota won the A.L. in 1965 before losing to the Los Angeles Dodgers in the World Series.

Future Hall of Famer Rod Carew, a Panamanian native who was a wizard with the bat, soon arrived in Minnesota, and the team won the first two A.L. West titles in 1969 and 1970. The Twins couldn't get past the Baltimore

ENCYCLOPEDIA OF BASEBALL

Orioles in the A.L. Championship Series, though, and the team's first World Series title in Minnesota would have to wait until 1987.

By then, the Twins were playing their home games in the Hubert H. Humphrey Metrodome, an indoor ballpark that gave them a big home-field advantage because of their noisy fans. Those fans cheered on stars such as outfielder Kirby Puckett and first baseman Kent Hrbek. Manager Tom Kelly's squad won Minnesota's first pennant in 22 years in 1987, then beat the St. Louis Cardinals in seven games—all four of the Twins' victories came at home—in the World Series.

The franchise has had dramatic swings in fortune ever since. By 1990, for instance, the Twins were a last-place team. In 1991, they went from worst to first, besting the Atlanta Braves in a dramatic seven-game World Series punctuated by memorable performances from Puckett in Game Six (he starred in the extra-inning game with a leaping catch at the wall and a game-winning home run) and pitcher Jack Morris in Game Seven (he threw a 10-inning, complete-game shutout).

By the end of the decade of the 1990s, Minnesota had the A.L.'s poorest record again. Soon, there was talk that the team would be dissolved. As a small-market franchise, it was having trouble competing with the big-market teams on the field and at the gate. But the Twins not only survived, they thrived. Left-hander Johan Santana turned into baseball's best pitcher, outfielder Torii Hunter became an All-Star, and Minnesota won 90 or more games three years in a row beginning in 2002. The 2006 team won 96 games and the club's fourth division title in five seasons.

Santana and Hunter have since moved on to other teams, but a host of new youngsters such as first baseman Justin Morneau (the 2006 A.L. MVP), outfielder Carlos Gomez, and catcher Joe Mauer, along with pitchers Nick Blackburn and Scott Baker, have Twins' fans excited about the future—and the present.

■ *Outfielder Michael Cuddyer.*

MINNESOTA TWINS

LEAGUE: **AMERICAN**

DIVISION: **CENTRAL**

YEAR FOUNDED: **1901**

CURRENT COLORS:
NAVY BLUE AND RED

STADIUM (CAPACITY):
HUBERT H. HUMPHREY METRODOME (45,423)

ALL-TIME RECORD
(THROUGH 2008):
8,051–8,672

WORLD SERIES TITLES
(MOST RECENT): **3 (1991)**

51

■ *Miller's work still has a huge effect on baseball.*

A veteran labor organizer who once fought for the United Steelworkers Union, Miller was hired by the players in 1966. Two years later, he negotiated the MLBPA's first collective bargaining agreement with the team owners. A collective bargaining agreement, or CBA, means workers come together to negotiate terms of employment that affect all the workers together. Baseball's 1968 CBA featured the first increase in the sport's minimum salary in 20 years.

The players loved Miller. He eventually fought for–and won–many other changes, most notably limited free agency and salary arbitration. (Arbitration means that both sides in a disagreement agree to let an independent person make the final decision for them.) Miller was not always popular with baseball fans, however, because his work led to several players' strikes or owners' lockouts in the 1970s and 1980s. He is not in the Hall of Fame, but many baseball experts feel he deserves the honor.

Milwaukee Braves

Milwaukee Braves is the name under which the Atlanta Braves played from 1953 to 1965. The club was an original member of the National League in 1876 in Boston. It was known by several different names, including Braves, before taking the name for good in 1941. In 1966, the Braves moved to Atlanta.

For a complete history of the franchise, please see Atlanta Braves.

Milwaukee Brewers

The Milwaukee Brewers were an original member of the American League in 1901. The next season, the team moved to St. Louis and became the Browns. In 1954, the Browns moved to Baltimore and became the Orioles.

For a complete history of this franchise, please see Baltimore Orioles. For the current Milwaukee Brewers, see pages 48–49.

Minnesota Twins

Please see pages 50–51.

Minor Leagues

 The minor leagues are the various levels of professional baseball that serve as the training ground for Major-League players. The purpose is to identify and develop players who can be ready as needed to join the big-league team.

The highest minor leagues are classified as the AAA level. Other levels include AA, A, and Rookie. As late as the 1950s and early 1960s, there were additional levels B, C, and D. But those levels are no longer in use because the total number of minor leagues now is about 20—far fewer than the all-time high of 60.

Most minor-league teams are independently owned and operated but have a working agreement with a Major-League team. The Louisville team in the International League, for instance, is the AAA affiliate of the Cincinnati Reds.

Mitt

Mitt is sometimes used as another name for any fielder's glove, but usually it is reserved for the special gloves worn by catchers and first basemen. Those gloves have one section for the thumb and one for four fingers, with the original designs giving them the shape of a mitten.

Molitor, Paul

Paul Molitor's induction into the Hall of Fame in 2004 was a tribute to his versatility and dependability. In 21 big-league seasons with the Milwaukee Brewers (1978–1992), Toronto Blue Jays (1993–95), and Minnesota Twins (1996–98), Molitor amassed 3,319 hits and stole 504 bases while playing every position except pitcher and catcher. He spent his later years as an effective designated hitter.

Molitor was a lifetime .306 hitter. He never won a batting title, but he placed among the A.L.'s top-10 hitters 11 times and earned seven All-Star selections. He hit a career-best .353 in 1987 and, although not a power hitter, drove in more than 100 runs two times. In 1996, the season he turned 40 years old, he batted .341 and drove in a career-best 113 runs despite hitting only nine home runs.

■ *A catcher's mitt is hinged at the bottom.*

Molitor helped the 1982 Brewers and the 1993 Blue Jays to A.L. pennants. He had a record five hits in Game One of the '82 Series, then hit .500 to earn MVP honors in Toronto's six-game victory over Philadelphia in '93.

Montreal Expos

The Montreal Expos were an expansion team that began play in 1969.

■ *Morgan was the engine of the Big Red Machine.*

The Expos played in Montreal through the 2004 season before moving to Washington, D.C., and becoming the Nationals.

For a complete history of the franchise, please see Washington Nationals.

Morgan, Joe

Joe Morgan was a Hall-of-Fame second baseman who played for five Major-League teams in a 22-season career from 1963 to 1984. He was a member of Cincinnati's "Big Red Machine" in the 1970s, and played a pivotal role on the '75 Reds' team that beat the Boston Red Sox in one of the greatest World Series ever.

"Little Joe" stood only 5 feet 7 inches tall, but he packed a punch on his 160-pound frame. He belted 268 home runs in his career, including 27 in 1976. That year, despite playing in a lineup loaded with superstars such as Johnny Bench, Pete Rose, and Tony Perez, it was Morgan, who batted .320 while driving in 111 runs, that earned N.L. MVP honors for the second consecutive year. In the World Series, he hit .333 during the Reds' four-game sweep of the Yankees. The year before, it was Morgan who delivered the go-ahead single in the top of the ninth inning of Cincinnati's 4–3 victory over Boston in Game Seven.

Morgan, a heady player with a competitive fire to match, is now a noted analyst on televised baseball games. He was a 10-time All-Star and five-time Gold Glove winner.

His 689 career steals—including 60 or more in three seasons—ranked 11th on the big-leagues' all-time list through 2008.

Morneau, Justin

Justin Morneau is the left-handed-hitting first baseman for the Minnesota Twins. He was the American League's Most Valuable Player for 2006.

Morneau played parts of two seasons before becoming a full-time starter for the first time in 2005. He belted 22 home runs that year but hit only .239 before breaking out the next year. In 2006, he batted .321 with 34 homers and 130 RBI. He made the All-Star Game for the first time in '07, when he hit 31 homers and drove in 111 runs.

Morneau is a native of Canada who was drafted by the Twins out of high school in the third round in 1999. He was the second Canadian to win an MVP award after Larry Walker, who was the N.L. choice while with the Colorado Rockies in 1997.

■ *Morneau is one of several young stars for the Twins.*

Most Valuable Player

The Most Valuable Player Award, often shortened to MVP, is an official Major League Baseball award presented to the outstanding player in each league.

Since 1931, the A.L. and N.L. MVPs have been determined in a vote by the Baseball Writers Association of America. Some form of the award, however, has existed since 1911, when the Chalmers Award (sponsored by the Chalmers Motor Company) first was handed out. There were no official MVPs from 1915 to 1921, none in 1930, and no A.L. MVP in 1929.

Outfielder Barry Bonds is the only player to win more than three league MVP

continued on page 58

Movies, Baseball and

Movies about baseball have been around almost as long as movies have been made. Hundreds of films with a direct connection to the sport have been made since Thomas Edison released *The Ball Game*—a documentary featuring a New Jersey team played against an unknown opponent—in 1898. Baseball has such a long and storied history in motion pictures, in fact, that in 2006, the Hall of Fame began holding an annual Baseball Film Festival in Cooperstown. The Hall of Fame Library also includes an exhibit on "Baseball at the Movies."

Most baseball films can be categorized as "biopics" or as fiction. Biopics dramatize the lives of real characters (in this case, baseball players); the most famous of these is probably *The Pride of the Yankees*, the 1942 film depicting the life of Yankees legend Lou Gehrig. Gary Cooper played the lead role. Babe Ruth, Gehrig's famous teammate, played himself in several scenes.

Ruth's own life was put on the big screen many times, with the most famous being 1948's *The Babe Ruth*

■ *Babe Ruth (left) with movie star Gary Cooper as Lou Gehrig.*

Story, starring William Bendix as the "Sultan of Swat." Later versions, such as 1992's *The Babe*, starring John Goodman, were more realistic about including both the good and the bad about Ruth's life.

Future President Ronald Reagan played pitcher Grover Cleveland Alexander in 1952's *The Winning Team*; Anthony Perkins was Jimmy Piersall in 1957's *Fear Strikes Out*; and Dan Dailey played Dizzy Dean in 1952's *The Pride of St. Louis*.

Some more recent films have also dramatized real events, such as *Eight Men Out* (1988; the 1919 Black Sox Scandal) and *A League of Their Own* (1992; the All-American Girls Professional Baseball League). A 2002 movie called *The Rookie*, based on the short, but unlikely, career of a pitcher, became a very popular baseball movie.

The most successful baseball films, though, have been works of complete fiction. These might include real players, but the plot is strictly a story, such as 1989's *Field of Dreams*. *The Natural* (1984) and *Bull Dur-*

■ *Dennis Quaid (left) played pitcher Jim Morris in* **The Rookie.**

ham (1988) join *Field of Dreams* on almost every "Best Baseball Movie" list. (Note: Some of these movies are rated PG or above. Make sure you ask your parents before watching.)

Some fun baseball movies aimed at kids include *Rookie of the Year* (1993), in which a kid joins the Chicago Cubs as a pitcher; *The Sandlot* (1993), about a group of kids, a valuable baseball, and a mean dog; and *Angels in the Outfield* (1994), about a team that gets some heavenly help to win.

■ *Pitchers stand atop the dirt mound to throw.*

awards. He was named the best player in the N.L. seven times in a 15-season span from 1990 to 2004.

MVP awards are also given to the outstanding player of various special events, such as the World Series, ALCS, NLCS, or the All-Star Game.

Mound

The mound is the raised dirt surface from which the pitcher throws the ball to home plate. By rule, it can be no more than 10 inches at its highest point. (It was

lowered to that height in 1969 after pitchers so dominated play that rules makers wanted to help hitters out.)

The pitching rubber–the white, 6-inch by 24-inch (15 by 60 cm) slab that the pitcher must be touching when he throws the ball–is placed in the center of the mound, 60 feet 6 inches (18.4 m) from the plate.

Movies, Baseball and

Please see pages 56–57.

Murray, Eddie

"Steady Eddie" Murray never was the flashiest player in baseball. But in 21 seasons for five teams from 1977 to 1997, he consistently produced at such a high level that he was inducted into the Hall of Fame in his first year of eligibility in 2003.

Murray made his debut as a 21-year-old first baseman and designated hitter for the Baltimore Orioles in 1977. He earned league Rookie-of-the-Year honors that season after hitting 27 home runs. He would go on to belt at least 20 homers, but no more than 33, in 16 seasons. In 1978, Murray earned the first of eight career All-Star selections. Five years later, he batted .306 with 33 homers and 111 RBI for the Orioles' World Series champs.

For his career, Murray batted .287 with 3,255 hits, including 504 homers. His 1,917 RBI still ranked ninth on the all-time list entering 2009.

Musial, Stan

Sweet-swinging Stan Musial was one of the best hitters in baseball history. In 22 seasons with the St. Louis Cardinals from 1941 to 1963 (he didn't play in 1945 while serving in the military), "Stan the Man" hit .331 with 475 home runs. His 3,630 career hits rank fourth among all players in big-league history.

Musial, a converted minor-league pitcher who played left field and first base in the Majors, ranked at or near the top in many offensive categories at the time of his retirement. He belted 725 doubles, scored 1,949 runs, and drove in 1,951 runs. He played in 24 All-Star Games (two games were played each year from 1959 to 1962) and four World Series (the Cardinals won three of them).

Musial was a seven-time batting champ who finished among the top 10 in N.L. MVP balloting an astounding 14 times. He won the award three times, with the last coming in 1948. That year, he established career bests with a .376 average, 39 home runs, and 131 RBI. He was just one home run short of winning the league Triple Crown that season.

Elected to the Hall of Fame in 1969, Musial's success on the field and his gentlemanly charm off of it have made him one of the most famous and popular athletes in St. Louis history. He was named to baseball's All-Century Team in 1999.

Mussina, Mike

Mike Mussina has had nearly two decades of success as a starting pitcher. He is the only pitcher in big-league history with at least 10 wins in 17 straight seasons.

"Moose," a five-time All-Star, got to his career total of 270 wins entering 2009 by being remarkably consistent and durable. At age 39 in 2008, the Yankees' right-hander was a 20-game winner for the first time.

■ *Mussina has been a steady winner for 17 years.*

■ *The Santa Barbara Foresters are two-time NBC champions.*

National Baseball Congress World Series

The National Baseball Congress (NBC) World Series is held each summer in Wichita, Kansas. It matches the top summer-league teams from across the country. It was first played in 1937 and has featured some of the greatest players in baseball history, from Satchel Paige and Mickey Mantle to Barry Bonds and Roger Clemens.

Summer-league teams were originally semipro or amateur teams from small towns, mostly in the Midwest. Today, most NBC-level teams play in college summer leagues, using players who are on summer break from college, and junior-college squads. Teams travel to Wichita from all over—Alaska, California, Michigan, Massachusetts, Illinois, and Kansas.

An example of a good NBC-level team is the Santa Barbara (Calif.) Foresters, who finished in the top four of the NBC World Series tournament every year from 2003–2008, including titles in 2006 and 2008.

National Commission

This was baseball's ruling body organized in 1903 to help make peace between the National and American Leagues. The members of the commission were

National Association

The National Association was formed in 1871 when 10 top baseball clubs met in New York on March 17 to form baseball's first "major" league. The teams agreed to play at least five games against each of the other teams. Teams were based in Boston, Chicago, Cleveland, Fort Wayne, New York, Philadelphia, Rockford, Troy, and Washington, D.C.

Some of the biggest stars that played in the National Association included Cap Anson and Al Spalding. Spalding, who later co-founded the sporting goods store that made his name famous to this day, joined the Boston Red Stockings in 1871 and won more than 200 games. Anson was one of the first stars of professional baseball, and the best batter in the early 1870s.

Harry Pulliam, president of the National League; Ban Johnson, president of the American League; and August Herrmann, president of the Cincinnati Reds and the Commission chairman.

In 1920, the three-man commission was replaced by a single, all-powerful commissioner, a former federal judge hired by the owners named Kenesaw Mountain Landis.

National League

In 1876, Chicago businessman William A. Hulbert and seven other owners formed the National League of Professional Baseball Clubs. Eventually, the new organization simply called itself the National League. It consisted of teams in Boston, Chicago, Cincinnati, Hartford, Louisville, New York, Philadelphia, and St. Louis. Of the original eight teams, only Boston (now the Atlanta Braves), Chicago, and Cincinnati are still in the National League today.

National League Championship Series (NLCS)

A second-round playoff series between the two winning N.L. Division Series teams. The winner captures the National League pennant, and goes on to the World Series against the winner of the ALCS. The first NLCS was held in 1969. The Atlanta Braves have appeared in the most NLCS competitions.

National League Division Series (NLDS)

A first-round playoff series between the three National League division winners and the wild-card winner (the second-place team with the best record). The two winning teams go on to the National League Championship Series (NLCS). The first official NLDS was played in 1995 after baseball reorganized into two leagues of

continued on page 64

■ *Upstart Colorado beat Arizona in the 2007 NLCS.*

Negro Leagues

Professional baseball leagues sprung up in the United States in the 1870s. During the early years, a number of African-American ballplayers played alongside white players. In the 1890s, however, the various professional leagues gradually pushed African-Americans out of organized baseball. They put up what was sometimes called the "color line."

However, many black players still wanted to play the game they loved, so they formed teams of their own to play each other. Rube Foster was the organizer and businessman behind the growing success of many black baseball teams in this era. He is often referred to as the "Father of Black Baseball." He organized the top Midwestern black clubs to form the Negro National League, and served as league president. (Editor's note: In those days, it was considered okay to refer to African-Americans as "Negroes." Today, however, that word should not be used except to describe historical events such as the Negro Leagues.) Also in 1920, Thomas T. Wilson, owner of the Nashville Elite Giants, organized the Negro Southern League with teams in Nashville, Atlanta, Birmingham, Memphis, Montgomery, and New Orleans. Three years later, the Eastern Colored League was formed featuring the Hilldale Club, Cuban Stars (East), Brooklyn Royal Giants, Bacharach Giants, Lincoln Giants, and Baltimore Black Sox.

The Negro National League was dominant throughout the 1920s, but dissolved after the 1931 season. The second Negro National League, organized by Pittsburgh bar owner Gus Greenlee, became the

■ *Star player Buck O'Neil with a statue of "Cool Papa" Bell.*

dominant force in black baseball from 1933 through 1949. Greenlee's Pittsburgh Crawfords assembled a team in 1935 with five future Hall of Famers: Satchel Paige, Josh Gibson, Cool Papa Bell, Judy Johnson, and Oscar Charleston.

One of the biggest myths about the Negro Leagues is that there aren't any definitive sources of information about their players. Since the early 1990s, there are several books that list stats and yearly chronicles of league play.

The Complete Book of the Negro Leagues: The Other Half of Baseball History, written by historian John Holway, goes into great detail on Negro League seasons, records, postseason games, and match-ups against the best white stars. Holway has been researching baseball since 1944. He and author and fellow historian James A. Riley are among the nation's most knowledgeable experts of Negro League baseball.

After Jackie Robinson joined the Brooklyn Dodgers to integrate the Major Leagues in 1947, the popularity of the Negro Leagues faded. By the early 1960s, there were no more Negro League teams. Their legacy lives on through the surviving players and through the Negro Leagues Baseball Museum, which opened in 1997 in Kansas City, where Foster and fellow owners organized the Negro National League in 1920.

■ *The famous Satchel Paige.*

three divisions each. In 1981, the playoffs included an extra round when a players' strike interrupted the season. That round is included in NLDS records and history.

The American League also has its own Division Series (ALDS).

■ *"Prince Hal" was a big winner in the 1940s.*

Newhouser, Hal

Hal Newhouser was the dominant left-handed pitcher during wartime baseball in the 1940s, winning the American League Most Valuable Player award in 1944 and 1945 (and finishing second to Ted Williams in 1946). He made his debut for the Detroit Tigers at age 18 in 1939 and pitched for them until 1953, ending his career as a reliever for the Cleveland Indians two years later. Newhouser won 207 games in his career, but more than 90 percent of them came before his 30th birthday.

In 1944, Newhouser won 29 games with a 2.22 earned run average to capture his first MVP award. In 1945, Newhouser won 25 games with a 1.81 ERA. He led the Tigers to the American League pennant, and then pitched complete-game victories in Games Five and Seven of the World Series to lead the Tigers to the championship. In 1946, he won 26 games.

"Prince Hal" had his best seasons during World War II, when many of the top-line players were fighting overseas. The sentiment that Newhouser didn't dominate the competition at full strength probably delayed his Hall-of-Fame enshrinement. He was elected to the Hall by the Veterans Committee in 1992. He was the first Tigers' pitcher ever elected to the Hall.

New York Giants

The Giants were formed in the early 1880s and were one of the first and most successful teams of the modern National League. (They moved to San Francisco in 1958; this section describes highlights of their years in New York. See San Francisco Giants for more information.)

The New York Giants dominated the N.L. from 1903 to the beginning of the 1930s, thanks in large part to their legendary manager John McGraw. The man known as "Little Napoleon" was synonymous with the New York Giants. In 29 seasons and parts of two others, McGraw led the Giants to 10 pennants, 11 second-place finishes, and six other years in the first division. Giants' ownership (and manager McGraw) wouldn't play the Red Sox—champions of the junior American League—in the World Series in 1904 because they so hated what they considered a minor league. McGraw and the Giants changed their tune a year later.

McGraw had some of the greatest players in history at his disposal, including pitcher Christy Mathewson. Mathewson used his "fadeaway" pitch to win at least 30 games in four seasons. In the 1905 World Series, he threw 27 innings of shutout ball.

In the waning days of the 1908 pennant race, the Giants were facing the Cubs on September 23. The score was 1–1 heading into the bottom of the ninth. New York had

■ *Giants pitcher "King" Carl Hubbell.*

runners on first and third with two outs, when 18-year old Fred Merkle (running from first base) failed to touch second as the winning run from third scored. Merkle was ruled out, the run was taken away, and the game called on account of darkness. A century later, it is remembered as "Merkle's Mistake." The Giants finished the season tied with the Cubs and lost the "replayed" game of September 23 to Chicago.

First baseman Bill Terry was a lifetime .341 batter for the Giants, and hit .401

continued on page 70

New York Mets

When the National League's New York Giants and Brooklyn Dodgers both left for California following the 1957 season, it left a gaping hole in New York's baseball landscape. In 1962, the National League expanded with new teams in Houston and New York. The largest city in the United States returned to the National League with a team known as the Mets (short for Metropolitans).

The Mets hired former Yankees manager Casey Stengel as their first manager. The 1962 Mets were entertaining—and horren-

■ *Wright is one of MLB's top young hitters.*

dous. They finished 40–120, more than 60 games out of first place. But they improved, and by the end of the decade, they shocked the world. Under the steady hand of manager Gil Hodges, the franchise turned around when a young pitcher named Tom Seaver came on the scene in 1967. After finishing ninth in 1968, the "Miracle Mets" went from 73 wins that season to 100 in 1969. The Mets won the '69 World Series, upsetting the heavily favored Baltimore Orioles. In 1973, the Mets found themselves in last place as late as the end of August. Relief ace Tug McGraw coined a rallying cry ("Ya gotta believe!"), and the Mets rallied to win the pennant, only to lose a tough seven-game World Series to the Oakland A's.

Seaver became the Mets' first Hall of Famer in 1992. "Tom Terrific" was the best player in the first 40 years of the franchise's history, but he only played 10 seasons with New York. He was traded in mid-season 1977 in a controversial move that came in the beginning years of free-agency.

The Mets bottomed out at the end of the 1970s, and the team's fortunes improved when they selected Darryl Strawberry with the No. 1 overall pick in the 1980 amateur draft. Strawberry was the Rookie of the Year in 1983. A 1982 draft pick—pitcher Dwight Gooden—became the 1984 Rookie of the Year. The two led the Mets to the 1986 World

Series championship. It didn't come easy, as the Mets faced elimination in Game Six. They were within an out of losing the Series to the ill-fated Boston Red Sox. But the Mets got a couple of hits and a wild pitch to tie the game, then won it when Mookie Wilson's ground ball trickled through first baseman Bill Buckner's legs. New York won Game Seven two nights later.

The Mets haven't won a World Series since then, even though they have come close to a championship several times:

➤ In 1988, the Mets won 100 games and lost the NLCS to the Los Angeles Dodgers, a team they had defeated 10 of 11 times during the regular season.

➤ In 1999, the Mets—trailing the Atlanta Braves 0–3 in games in the NLCS—rallied to win Games Four and Five. They lost Game Six in 11 innings.

➤ In 2000, the Mets made it back to the Fall Classic, but they lost a Subway Series to the Yankees in five games.

➤ In 2006, the Mets won the National League East title, then beat the Dodgers in the Division Series. But they lost

■ *First baseman Carlos Delgado.*

Game Seven of the NLCS at home to the St. Louis Cardinals.

➤ In 2007, the Mets led their division by seven games with only 17 games remaining in the regular season. But they faltered down the stretch and failed to even qualify for the postseason.

Those have been some frustrating times for the Mets and for their fans. But they hope that their move to a new ballpark in 2009—the Mets left Shea Stadium for new Citi Field—will bring a new era of success.

NEW YORK METS

LEAGUE: **NATIONAL**

DIVISION: **EAST**

YEAR FOUNDED: **1962**

CURRENT COLORS:
BLACK, BLUE, AND ORANGE

STADIUM (CAPACITY):
CITI FIELD (45,000)

ALL-TIME RECORD
(THROUGH 2008):
3,585–3,889

WORLD SERIES TITLES
(MOST RECENT):
2 (1986)

New York Yankees

The New York Yankees won more World Series championships in the 20th century than any other Major-League club. They are, by far, the most successful franchise in history.

In 1901, the Baltimore Orioles were one of eight original franchises in the American League. Two years later, the team moved to New York and became the Highlanders. In

■ *"Joltin' Joe" DiMaggio.*

1913, the Highlanders changed their name to the Yankees. In 1915, pinstripes first appeared on the team's uniforms. The man who filled out the pinstripes best, Babe Ruth, was purchased from the Red Sox in 1920 (for $125,000 and a $350,000 loan secured by a mortgage on Fenway Park). "The Bambino," as Ruth was known, paid off right away. In 1920, when Ruth hit more home runs than any other A.L. team, the Yankees drew 1,289,422 fans, a big-league record that would stand for 26 years (until 1946).

The Yankees won their first pennant in 1921. It was their first of 29 pennants and 20 World Series championships in the 44 seasons between 1921 and 1964. Some of baseball's most memorable streaks, records, and achievements were recorded by Yankees' players in this era. Ruth hit 60 home runs in 1927, a mark that stood 34 years. Lou Gehrig had an ironman streak of 2,130 consecutive games played, a record for 56 years. And Joe DiMaggio hit in 56 consecutive games in 1941, a record that still stands nearly 70 years later.

The Yankees had an abundance of talent starting with Ruth, a player many consider the greatest to ever play the game. His most memorable home run was his "called shot" in the fifth inning of Game Three of the 1932 World Series against the Chicago Cubs— although Ruth's intention remains unclear.

Was he pointing to a spot in center field where his shot would land? Or to the Cubs' bench to answer its relentless taunting? Ruth played two more seasons after that with New York, but by the early 1930s, it was Lou Gehrig who was New York's greatest player.

Gehrig is generally regarded as the greatest first baseman in history, and would be so noted even if not for his incredible durability. After Gehrig was finally forced out of the lineup early in 1939 due to an incurable disease, the Yankees declared July 4, 1939 as Lou Gehrig Day, and the club honored him between games of a doubleheader. His moving speech will never be forgotten. He died two years later.

Joe DiMaggio arrived on the Yankees in 1936, and he was no worse than the second- or third-best player of his generation—and one of the best and most graceful outfielders of all time. The Yankees won the World Series in each of his first four seasons.

When DiMaggio's career began to decline due to age and a series of heel injuries, young Mickey Mantle was ready to assume his place in the dynasty. The Yankees didn't just feature great slug-gers, though. Pitcher Whitey Ford anchored the staff throughout the 1950s and early '60s. And a journeyman, Don Larsen, would pitch a perfect game in Game Five of the 1956 World Series.

After 1964, the team slid into the second division for about 10 years. But in 1973, a Cleveland shipbuilder named George Steinbrenner bought the team. The Yankees won the World Series in both '77 and '78, with star slugger Reggie Jackson leading the way.

The Yankees didn't win another World Series until 1996, but by then they had begun another great run of success. They made 13 consecutive postseason appearances from 1995 to 2007. New York won the World Series in 1996, 1998, 1999, and 2000. These teams were led by relief ace Mariano Rivera, perhaps the greatest closer ever; and by shortstop Derek Jeter, one of the biggest stars of his generation.

■ *Matsui: from Japan to New York.*

NEW YORK YANKEES
LEAGUE: **AMERICAN**
DIVISION: **EAST**
YEAR FOUNDED: **1901**
CURRENT COLORS: **NAVY BLUE AND WHITE**
STADIUM (CAPACITY): **YANKEE STADIUM (52,325)**
ALL-TIME RECORD (THROUGH 2008): **9,472–7,235**
WORLD SERIES TITLES (MOST RECENT): **26 (2000)**

in 1930, the last time a National Leaguer batted .400. Outfielder Mel Ott had an unusual left-handed batting stance (kicking his right leg up before hitting the ball) and used the short right-field of the Polo Grounds to hit a (then) National League-record 511 homers.

Left-handed pitcher Carl Hubbell made his debut in 1928. "King Carl" had a wicked screwball. His most famous feat came in the 1934 All Star game, only the second ever played. In that game, Hubbell struck out five future Hall of Famers in a row: Babe Ruth, Lou Gehrig, Al Simmons, Jimmie Foxx, and Joe Cronin.

"The Miracle at Coogan's Bluff" occurred in 1951. The Giants, led by their fiery manager Leo Durocher, were 13½ games behind Brooklyn on August 11. The Giants played incredible baseball down the stretch to finish in a first-place tie with the Dodgers and force a three-game playoff. The teams split the first two games. In the third game, the Dodgers led 4–1 entering the bottom of the ninth.

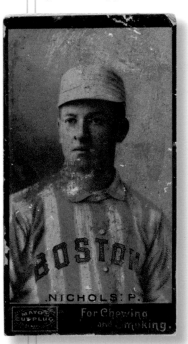

■ *Star pitcher Kid Nichols was nicknamed for his youthful appearance.*

After one run was in, Bobby Thomson hit a three-run home run, forever known as "The Shot Heard 'Round the World." New York announcer Russ Hodges famously shouted, "The Giants win the pennant! The Giants win the pennant! The Giants win the pennant!"

The Giants wouldn't have made their move in 1951 without rookie outfielder Willie Mays. Mays is considered one of the greatest all-around players ever. In the 1954 World Series, Mays made the signature play of his brilliant career. "The Catch" was an unlikely over-the-shoulder grab to rob Vic Wertz in the first game to shut down a Cleveland rally. The Giants went on to sweep the Indians.

The franchise moved to San Francisco following the 1957 season.

Nichols, Kid

Kid Nichols was one of the top pitchers in pro baseball's early years. In a career that began in 1890 and ended in 1906 (he didn't pitch in 1902 or '03), Nichols won 361 games, including 30 or more seven times in eight seasons beginning in 1891. And he almost always finished what he started: In 561 all-time starts, he tossed 531 complete games. He played most of his career with the Boston Beaneaters, whom he led to five N.L. titles in the 1890s. Nichols, whose real first name was Charles, was inducted into the Hall of Fame in 1949.

Niekro, Phil

There are spirited debates about which pitcher threw the best fastball, curveball, or splitter. But there are few experts that would argue about who threw the best and most consistent knuckleball. That would be Phil Niekro.

Niekro was a right-handed pitcher who lasted 24 years in the majors and won 318 games on the strength of his knuckler. He pitched for the Braves for 20 years. At the end of his career, he also pitched with the Yankees, Indians, and Blue Jays. Phil's younger brother, Joe, won 218 games in a 22-year career, making the Niekros the winningest brother combination in history.

The knuckleball made Phil Niekro extremely durable. He won 121 games after the age of 40. In 1979, at the age of 41, Nickro went 21–20 for the Braves, with a league-leading 23 complete games and 342 innings pitched. In 1985, at the age of 46, he won 16 games for the Yankees.

Phil Niekro pitched nearly a quarter-century in the Major Leagues, yet never advanced to the World Series. He succeeded, however, by throwing a pitch that danced in fluttering, unpredictable ways.

Niekro was inducted into the Hall of Fame in 1997.

■ *Phil Niekro's specialty was the knuckleball.*

Night Baseball

The Cincinnati Reds, in a move to increase ticket sales, installed lights at Crosley Field and staged the first seven night games in Major-League history in 1935. General manager Larry MacPhail's experiment was a success, as working people were able to attend games in greater numbers. By 1948, every big-league park except Chicago's Wrigley Field was illuminated. The Cubs held out for 40 years, but

■ *These days, most Major League Baseball games are played under the lights.*

finally installed lights. The first night baseball game at Wrigley Field was scheduled for August 8, 1988 (8-8-88). Following a rainout, the first night game at Wrigley was played the next night.

The first time lights were used in a World Series game was October 9, 1949. In the top of the ninth inning (at 4:50 P.M.) in the fifth and final game between the Dodgers and the Yankees, the lights were turned on at Ebbets Field in Brooklyn.

The first World Series game to be played entirely under the lights was October 13, 1971, in Pittsburgh. That was Game Four of the Series between the Pirates and the Baltimore Orioles. The first Series to be played with all night games was 1985.

The move to night baseball affected the Major Leagues in a number of ways. Attendance increased, as more fans were able to attend games without missing work. Television ratings (and rights fees) increased, for the same reason. This led to higher salaries by players. One negative is that games ended too late (on the East Coast) for young kids to attend or watch to completion.

No-hitter

When a pitcher or pitchers on the same team do not allow a base hit during a game. In slang, also called a "no-no." An official no-hit game occurs when a pitcher (or pitchers) allows no hits during the entire course of a game, which consists of at least nine innings.

There have been 17 games in Major-League history (through 2008) in which a pitcher (or pitchers) allowed no hits and no base runners. These are perfect games, the rarest of no-hitters. The last perfect game was thrown by Arizona's Randy Johnson in 2004.

Throughout baseball's history, there has been a superstition and etiquette concerning on-going no-hitters. It is thought to be a jinx to mention the no-hitter during the game, especially to the pitcher. Even broadcasters have gone to great lengths to state the obvious—one team has no hits—but in subtle ways.

Since 1899, there have been 243 no-hitters (in 109 seasons through 2008). That's 2.2 no-hitters per year. That includes the all-time record of seven thrown by Nolan Ryan (for three different teams). It also includes the "no-no's" in back-to-back starts by the

Cincinnati Reds' Johnny Vander Meer on June 11 and June 15, 1938.

Some no-hitters are more memorable than others. In 1940, Bob Feller of the Cleveland Indians pitched a no-hitter on Opening Day. In 1968, no-hitters were pitched on consecutive days in the same series (the Giants' Gaylord Perry against the Cardinals; the next day, the Cards' Ray Washburn against the Giants). In 1986,

■ *He did it! Boston's Jon Lester celebrates a no-hitter in 2008.*

NO-HITTER TRIVIA

MOST NO-HITTERS PITCHED: **NOLAN RYAN, 7**

MOST NO-HITTERS CAUGHT: **RAY SCHALK, 4**

MOST CONSECUTIVE HITLESS INNINGS: **CY YOUNG, 24**

FIRST PITCHER TO TOSS A NO-HITTER IN NATIONAL LEAGUE AND AMERICAN LEAGUE: **CY YOUNG**

FIRST NO-HITTER IN A DOME: **DON WILSON, HOUSTON ASTROS, 1969**

ONLY NO-HITTER IN A WORLD SERIES GAME:
DON LARSEN, N.Y. YANKEES, 1956 (PERFECT GAME)

ONLY PITCHER TO THROW A NO-HITTER IN HIS FIRST CAREER START (POST-1900 ERA):
BOBO HOLLOMAN, ST. LOUIS BROWNS, 1953

MOST ONE-HITTERS PITCHED: **BOB FELLER AND NOLAN RYAN, 12**

Mike Scott pitched a no-hitter to clinch a division title for the Astros.

There have been inspirational no-hitters, too, such as the Yankees' Jim Abbott, who was born without a right hand, no-hitting Cleveland in 1993.

The final no-hitter of the 2008 season came when Carlos Zambrano of the Cubs no-hit the Houston Astros in a game played in Milwaukee due to problems caused by Hurricane Ike in Houston.

A no-hitter can happen at any game, and fans are tuned into a great performance when a pitcher gets into the sixth or seventh without allowing a hit.

Nolan, Ed "The Only"

Some players earn fame through their skills and achievements on the field. Some become well-known for their charitable work or their courage. Then there are guys like Ed Nolan. He earned his place in this Encyclopedia, and in baseball history, for having a very interesting and cool nickname. He was "The Only" Nolan.

Nolan was a pitcher for five teams from 1878–1885. The source of his nickname has never really been nailed down. Some stories say it's from his big ego, as he wanted to be "the only."

Nomo, Hideo

Hideo Nomo threw two no-hitters in his Major-League career with seven different teams from 1995 to 2008. However, Nomo will be long remembered not for his no-hitters, or his other 121 victories in the Majors (more than 200 wins in all including his Nippon League seasons), but for his efforts to pave the way for Japanese ballplayers to play in the United States.

Nomo, born in Osaka in 1968, was a member of Japan's 1988 silver-medal Olympic team. Known as "The Tornado" for his sweeping windup, he played in Japan until 1994. Nomo and other Japanese players had so much to overcome besides the obvious language barrier to break into the Majors. There was an unspoken agreement that Japanese players would not jump to the U.S. Major Leagues, ever since a pitcher named Masanori Murakami pitched two years with the San Francisco Giants beginning in 1964. There were cultural barriers to overcome. There was a very restrictive reserve clause in Japan, binding players to their Japanese teams. Despite all this, Nomo and his agents found a loophole and signed with the Los Angeles Dodgers in 1995. Following his signing, it was reported that Nomo had been disowned by his family for disgracing them. They begged him to come home to Japan right away.

Nomo stayed in Los Angeles, and his success opened the floodgates for his fellow Japanese players. In a strike-shortened 1995 season, he won 13 games, led the league in strikeouts, and finished fourth in earned run average. He started the All-Star Game for the National

League, and finished fourth in the Cy Young Award voting. The next season, he won 16 games and again finished fourth in Cy Young voting. He would go on to have

■ *"The Tornado" had a unique pitching delivery.*

■ *No other Red Sox player will wear Fisk's No. 27.*

The honor of retiring numbers varies from club to club. Some clubs refuse to retire uniform numbers, choosing to remember their stars in other ways. In modern days, players often play for more than one franchise. Some greats have even had their number retired by more than one team. Hank Aaron (Braves, Brewers), Rod Carew (Twins and Angels), Rollie Fingers (A's and Brewers), Carlton Fisk (Red and White Sox), Reggie Jackson (A's and Yankees), Frank Robinson (Reds and Orioles), Nolan Ryan (Rangers, Astros, and Angels), and Casey Stengel (Yankees and Mets) are among them. And of course, on April 15, 1997, Major League Baseball retired the No. 42 to honor Jackie Robinson, meaning that no player on any Major League team could wear the number 42 (except for the handful of players that were then wearing the number).

The Yankees have the most retired uniform numbers with 16, honoring 17 different players.

a productive career but will be best remembered for being the first Japanese player in decades to play in the Major Leagues.

Numbers, Retired

In December, 1939, after the season in which Lou Gehrig took himself out of the lineup for the first time in 14 years, the Yankees retired his uniform number 4. It was the first number retirement in baseball history. That means that no player will ever again wear that number for the Yankees' team.

Numbers, Uniform

The Yankees were the first team to wear uniform numbers (1929), with the Cleveland Indians sporting numbers the same season. The Yankees originally assigned numbers by batting order, thus Babe Ruth was number 3 and Lou Gehrig number 4 for batting third and fourth.

By the 1932 season, both teams in the World Series wore numbers on their uniforms, and by the mid-30s, it was standard for all teams.

Certain numbers seem to signify certain types of players. The number 1 has usually been worn by smaller, leadoff batters—such Pee Wee Reese and Ozzie Smith—while 44 has been worn home-run hitters such as Willie McCovey, Hank Aaron, and Reggie Jackson. Two of the greatest third basemen wore number 5: Brooks Robinson and George Brett.

One player wore his birthday on his uniform. Outfielder Carlos May wore number 17 below the name on the back of his uniform—and his birthday was May 17!

Nuxhall, Joe

In 1944, Joe Nuxhall became the youngest player to appear in a Major League game in the modern era (post-1900). The left-handed pitcher was in high school and was only 15 years old when he appeared in relief for the Cincinnati Reds in a game against the St. Louis Cardinals. The Reds had room for him on the roster because many Major League players were serving in the military during World War II.

The teenager was overmatched in his first big-league appearance, al-lowing five runs in two-thirds of an inning, and he did not pitch again that season. He was back in the Majors by 1952. He went on to win 135 games in his career. His best season was in 1955, when he won 17 games and earned the first of back-to-back All-Star nods with the Reds.

Nuxhall retired following the 1966 season and became a Reds' broadcaster. He was in the booth for 38 seasons and became a Cincinnati icon. He passed away in 2007.

■ *Now batting for the Cubs, No. 12, Alfonso Soriano.*

Oakland Athletics

Please see pages 80–81.

Obstruction

 "The act of a fielder who, while not in possession of the ball and not in the act of fielding the ball, impedes [slows down] the progress of any runner." In other words, if a fielder gets in the way of a baserunner, the runner can be called safe. The umpire makes the call, usually immediately upon seeing the obstruction take place.

■ *Oh is baseball's all-time home-run champ.*

Official Scorer

An independent observer who provides an impartial and fair view of each play to determine how the play is to be recorded, such as hit, error, fielder's choice, etc. These scoring decisions become the official statistical record of baseball.

Off-speed Pitch

A pitch thrown with less velocity than the pitcher's usual fastball. Also called a changeup or change of pace. A pitcher who throws a successful off-speed pitch is said to "pull the string."

Oh, Sadaharu

Sadaharu Oh is the Japanese and world home-run record holder. He hit 868 homers in his Japan League professional career from 1959 to 1980. Oh played his entire career for the Yomiuri Giants, who were Japan's version of the New York Yankees—big winners.

Oh signed a contract with the Yomiuri Giants in 1959, at age 19, and the first baseman would lead the team to 11 championships. He was the Central League's Most Valuable Player nine times, and an All-Star 18 times.

In 1964, the slugging star set a Japanese single-season record with 55 home runs (Japan's season is shorter than that of the Major Leagues). He was the league's home-run king 15 times—including 13 seasons when he averaged 45 round-trippers per year. He was also a five-time batting champion, and he won consecutive Triple Crowns in 1973 and 1974. (A batting Triple Crown means leading the league in home runs, RBI, and batting average in the same season.)

In 1980, at age 40, Oh retired. In addition to his 868 home runs, he had 2,786 hits for a batting average of .301, with a Japanese-record 2,170 runs batted in. Oh became the manager of the Yomiuri Giants from 1984 to 1988, and later managed the Fukuoka Hawks to Japan Series championships in 1999 and 2003. In 2006, Oh managed the Japanese National Team to victory over Cuba in the World Baseball Classic.

Baseball experts have debated if Oh would have had success playing in the United States. Major Leaguers who played exhibition games in Japan during the 1960s and 1970s felt that Oh would have been a big star in the U.S. Former big-league player and manager Davey Johnson, who was a teammate of Hank Aaron (in the Majors with the Atlanta Braves) and Oh (in Japan), has said that Oh would have hit at least 700 home runs if he played in the Majors. Said Johnson: "Quality is still quality."

■ *The United States team celebrates its 2000 Olympic gold medal.*

Olympics, Baseball in the

Baseball was not part of the Olympics until it became a demonstration sport in 1984 at the Los Angeles Summer Games. That year, teams from Nicaragua, Canada, Korea, Japan, the Dominican Republic, Italy, and the United States competed. Cuba boycotted (refused to play in) the Games. Japan defeated the U.S. in the gold-medal game played at Dodger Stadium. The U.S.A. players that went on to the most successful Major-League careers from the 1984 Olympic team included Mark McGwire, Barry Larkin, and Will Clark.

In 1988, with the powerful Cuban team again boycotting the Games, the gold-medal game once again featured the U.S. against Japan. This time, the U.S. (led by

continued on page 82

Oakland Athletics

The Oakland Athletics (more commonly known as the A's) are the direct descendant of the Philadelphia Athletics, a charter member of the American League. The Athletics moved to Kansas City in 1955, and moved again to Oakland in 1968.

Owner Charles Finley ran a competitive ball club in a turbulent city in a turbulent time, and it worked. Finley had a mule for a mascot, paid players to grow facial hair, wanted to play with orange baseballs, and had many other colorful ideas. Finley's A's won three consecutive World Series championships (1972, 1973, 1974) while led by a trio

■ *Owner Charles Finley (center) and the A's were big winners in the 1970s.*

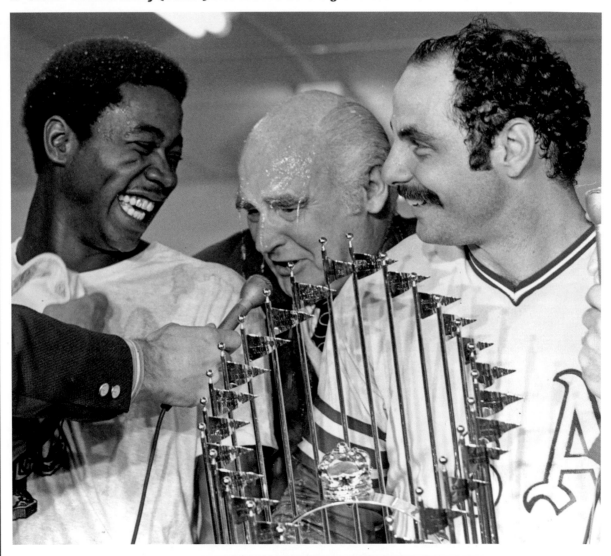

of future Hall of Famers: outfielder Reggie Jackson, pitcher Catfish Hunter, and relief ace Rollie Fingers. The core—which also included Vida Blue, Sal Bando, and Joe Rudi—might have played together longer, if not for the advent of free-agency in the mid-1970s. "The Swingin' A's" battled the cheap Finley as much as they battled their A.L. opponents.

Oakland fell to the bottom of the American League in the late '70s, after its best players were allowed to play out their contracts and leave. Finley revitalized the franchise in 1980 with the hiring of manager Billy Martin, but soon after was forced to sell the ball club he owned for 20 years. The A's won three A.L. West titles in a row starting in 1988, led by another Hall-of-Fame relief ace (Dennis Eckersley) and a pair of young sluggers. The "Bash Brothers" consisted of Jose Canseco and Mark McGwire. The A's were upset in the 1988 World Series by the Dodgers, won the 1989 Series (interrupted by a major earthquake in the Bay Area) in a sweep over the Giants, and were upset in the 1990 Series by the Reds.

Since the 1990 Series, the A's have made it to the postseason in 1992, 2000,

■ *Jack Cust had a breakout season in 2007.*

2001, 2002, 2003, and 2006. The A's have lost six of seven postseason series, winning only the Divisional Series round against Minnesota in 2006, before losing in the ALCS.

The A's have always been unconventional. In the early 2000s, they were among the most successful franchises despite having one of the lowest payrolls in baseball. They accomplished this with general manager Billy Beane's unique philosophy of player evaluation. The philosophy emphasized scouting players based on a position player's on-base percentage and a pitcher's strikeout-to-walk ratio.

OAKLAND ATHLETICS

LEAGUE: **AMERICAN**

DIVISION: **WEST**

YEAR FOUNDED: **1901**

CURRENT COLORS: **GREEN AND GOLD**

STADIUM (CAPACITY): **McAFEE COLISEUM (48,219)**

ALL-TIME RECORD (THROUGH 2008): **8,114–8,584**

WORLD SERIES TITLES (MOST RECENT): **9 (1989)**

Jim Abbott, Robin Ventura, and Tino Martinez) came out on top in what was still an unofficial part of the Olympics.

Baseball became an official Olympic sport in 1992. That year, Cuba did participate, and it took home the gold medal. Cuba defeated Japan to win gold again in 1996. Four years later, in one of the biggest surprises in Olympic history, Cuba was toppled in the gold-medal game in 2000 by an unheralded bunch of amateurs from the United States. Cuba won the gold medal in 2004, defeating Australia.

The 2008 gold-medal winner was South Korea, which defeated Cuba in the championship. South Korea might be the final Olympic baseball champion, however. In 2005, the International Olympic Committee (IOC) voted to remove baseball and softball from the Games starting in 2012. They were the first sports to be voted out of the Olympics since polo in 1936. Efforts to change that decision are ongoing.

On-base Percentage

A batter's number of hits plus walks plus times hit by a pitch divided by the number of at-bats plus walks plus times hit by a pitch plus sacrifices. An on-base percentage above .400 is very high.

On-deck Circle

A warm-up area near the dugout where a batter prepares for the next at-bat.

Opposite Field

Right field for a right-handed batter; left field for a left-handed batter.

Ortiz, David

With a big bat and an equally big personality, David Ortiz, also known as "Big Papi," helped the Boston Red Sox to a pair of World Series championships in the early 2000s.

Ortiz started his career with the Minnesota Twins, and signed as a free agent with the Red Sox after the 2002 season. Beginning in 2003, the left-handed batting Ortiz had one of the greatest five-year stretches in baseball history: He averaged 42 home runs, 128 RBI, and slugged .612. He finished in the top five in MVP voting his first five seasons with Boston. He might have won at least one MVP if he had not been a full-time DH.

Ortiz played a central role in the Red Sox's comeback from an 0–3 deficit in games in the 2004 American League Championship Series against the Yankees. Facing elimination in Game Four, Ortiz hit a walk-off home run in the bottom of the 12th inning. Facing elimination again in Game Five, Ortiz hit a game-tying home run in the bottom of the eighth, and a game-ending single with two outs in the bottom of the 14th. He was voted the ALCS MVP and helped the Red Sox win their first World Series in 86 years.

Ott, Mel

Mel Ott was one of the leading home-run hitters of his time, and one of the greatest sluggers in National League history. The lefty-swinging Ott was the first National Leaguer with 500 homers. Being left-handed was a big help, as he spent his entire 22-year career with the New York Giants. The team's Polo Grounds home park had a 260-foot-deep right field. Ott was known for lifting his right (front) foot before hitting the ball.

Giants manager John McGraw discovered Ott as a 16-year-old, and Ott became a regular three years later in 1925. When Ott retired in 1947, he was the all-time N.L. leader in homers, RBI, and runs. He played in three World Series for the Giants, all in the 1930s, winning one.

Ott managed the Giants from 1942 till mid-1948. In 1951, he was elected to the Baseball Hall of Fame. He worked as a broadcaster during the 1950s, until he was killed in an automobile accident in November 1958.

Out

Retiring a batter or runner by strikeout, force play, caught fly ball, or tag play. Three outs end a half-inning, and the teams change sides.

■ *"Big Papi" is one of baseball's most popular players.*

Outfield

The large, grassy area located beyond the infield. The outfield includes the area between the foul lines and inside the outfield walls.

Outfielder

One of three players who patrol the outfield: left fielder, center fielder, right fielder.

Keeping Score

It's a dying art, but it remains a great way to keep track of a baseball game. Keeping score means recording each play (or even each pitch) on a paper scoring chart like the one below. The key is to use the numbers for the positions (see box on page 13) and then other symbols to follow each batter's path around the bases. We've labeled this sample scorecard to show many of the plays that you might find—and write down—in a game.

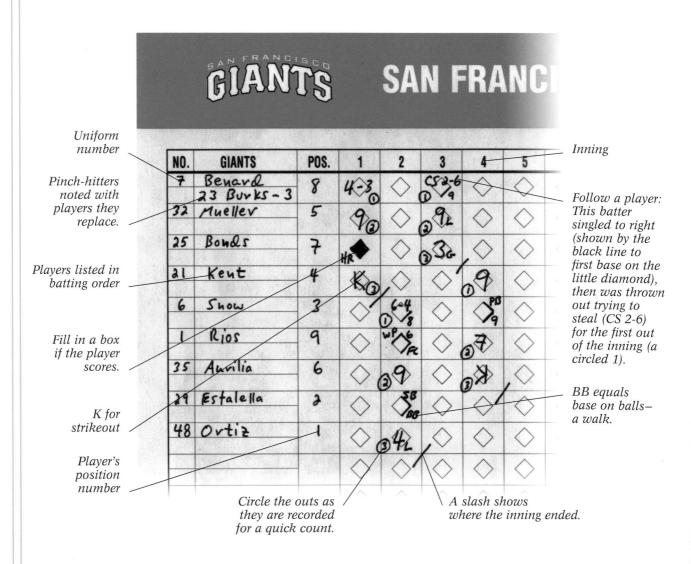

Uniform number

Pinch-hitters noted with players they replace.

Players listed in batting order

Fill in a box if the player scores.

K for strikeout

Player's position number

Inning

Follow a player: This batter singled to right (shown by the black line to first base on the little diamond), then was thrown out trying to steal (CS 2-6) for the first out of the inning (a circled 1).

BB equals base on balls— a walk.

Circle the outs as they are recorded for a quick count.

A slash shows where the inning ended.

Little League World Series

Just like in the Majors, Little League Baseball (see page 25) crowns its champion with a World Series each year. The winning teams came from these cities:

Year	Winner	Year	Winner
1947	Williamsport, Pennsylvania	1978	Pingtung, Taiwan
1948	Lock Haven, Pennsylvania	1979	Hsien, Taiwan
1949	Hammonton, New Jersey	1980	Hua-Lien, Taiwan
1950	Houston, Texas	1981	Taichung, Taiwan
1951	Stamford, Connecticut	1982	Kirkland, Washington
1952	Norwalk, Connecticut	1983	Marietta, Georgia
1953	Birmingham, Alabama	1984, 1985	Seoul, South Korea
1954	Schenectady, New York	1986	Tainan Park, Taiwan
1955	Morrisville, Pennsylvania	1987	Hua-Lien, Taiwan
1956	Roswell, New Mexico	1988	Taichung, Taiwan
1957, 1958	Monterrey, Mexico	1989	Trumbull, Connecticut
1959	Hamtramck, Michigan	1990	Tainan County, Taiwan
1960	Levittown, Pennsylvania	1991	Taichung, Taiwan
1961	El Cajon, California	1992, 1993	Long Beach, California
1962	San Jose, California	1994	Maracaibo, Venezuela
1963	Granada Hills, California	1995	Tainan, Taiwan
1964	Staten Island, New York	1996	Kaohsiung, Taiwan
1965	Windsor Locks, Connecticut	1997	Guadalupe, Mexico
1966	Houston, Texas	1998	Toms River, New Jersey
1967	West Tokyo, Japan	1999	Osaka, Japan
1968	Osaka, Japan	2000	Maracaibo, Venezuela
1969	Taipei, Taiwan	2001	Tokyo, Japan
1970	Wayne, New Jersey	2002	Louisville, Kentucky
1971	Tainan, Taiwan	2003	Tokyo, Japan
1972	Taipei, Taiwan	2004	Willemstad, Curacao
1973	Tainan City, Taiwan	2005	Ewa Beach, Hawaii
1974	Kaohsiung, Taiwan	2006	Columbus, Georgia
1975	Lakewood, New Jersey	2007	Warner Robins, Georgia
1976	Tokyo, Japan	2008	Waipio, Hawaii
1977	Kaohsiung, Taiwan		

Let's Go to the Movies!

Baseball has a long history on the big screen (see page 56). Here are some popular baseball movies. They are rated G or PG, but be sure to get an adult's permission before renting these movies or checking them out from your local library.

Title	Year	Title	Year
Air Bud: Seventh Inning Fetch	2002	The Kid from Left Field	1953
Angels in the Infield#	2000	The Kid From Left Field	1979
Angels in the Outfield#	1994	A League Of Their Own#	1992
Angels in the Outfield	1951	Little Big League#	1994
The Babe Ruth Story	1948	A Little Inside#	1999
Babe, The#	1992	Mickey#	2004
The Bad News Bears Go To Japan#	1978	The Natural#	1984
The Bad News Bears in Breaking Training#	1977	Pastime#	1991
		Perfect Game#	2000
The Bad News Bears (1976)#	1976	The Perfect Game	2008
Bang The Drum Slowly#	1973	The Pride of St. Louis	1952
The Bingo Long Traveling All-Stars & Motor Kings#	1976	Pride of the Yankees	1942
		Rookie of the Year#	1993
Blue Skies Again#	1983	The Rookie	2002
Damn Yankees!	1958	Safe at Home!	1962
Ed#	1996	Sandlot 2#	2005
Eight Men Out#	1988	Sandlot 3: Head for Home#	2007
Everyone's Hero	2006	The Sandlot#	1993
Fear Strikes Out	1957	The Stratton Story	1949
Field of Dreams#	1989	Talent for the Game#	1991
Final Season, The#	2007	Tiger Town	1983
Finding Buck McHenry#	2000	A Winner Never Quits#	1986
It Happens Every Spring	1949	The Winning Season#	2004
The Jackie Robinson Story	1950	# rated PG	

Retired Numbers

There's no greater honor for a player than to have his uniform number retired by his club (see page 76). Here are a few facts and figures about retired numbers.

Jackie Robinson's 42

Jackie Robinson is the only player whose uniform number has been retired throughout Major League Baseball. In 1997, to commemorate the 50th anniversary of Robinson's arrival in the big leagues—the African-American star broke baseball's color barrier that year—MLB announced that no other player would ever wear uniform number 42 again (right).

Elite Eight

Eight men have had their uniform numbers retired by more than one team. One of those eight, Hall-of-Fame pitcher Nolan Ryan, had his uniform number retired by three different franchises. These are the "elite eight."

Player or Manager	Uniform Number	Retired By
Hank Aaron	44	Atlanta Braves, Milwaukee Brewers
Rod Carew	29	Minnesota Twins, California Angels
Rollie Fingers	34	Oakland Athletics, Milwaukee Brewers
Carlton Fisk	27	Boston Red Sox
	72	Chicago White Sox
Reggie Jackson	9	Oakland Athletics
	44	New York Yankees
Frank Robinson	20	Cincinnati Reds, Baltimore Orioles
Nolan Ryan	30	California Angels
	34	Houston Astros, Texas Rangers
Casey Stengel	37	New York Yankees, New York Mets

Read the index this way: "4:62" means Volume 4, page 62.

Major League Baseball

Here's an easy way to find your favorite teams in the volumes of this encyclopedia. The numbers after each team's name below indicate the volume and page on which the information can be found. For instance, 1:14 means Volume 1, page 14.

American League

East Division		Central Division		West Division	
Baltimore Orioles	1:24	Chicago White Sox	1:62	Los Angeles Angels of Anaheim	3:26
Boston Red Sox	1:42	Cleveland Indians	1:68	Oakland Athletics	3:80
New York Yankees	3:68	Detroit Tigers	2:8	Seattle Mariners	4:52
Tampa Bay Rays	5:6	Kansas City Royals	3:14	Texas Rangers	5:10
Toronto Blue Jays	5:16	Minnesota Twins	3:50		

National League

East Division		Central Division		West Division	
Atlanta Braves	1:18	Chicago Cubs	1:60	Arizona Diamondbacks	1:14
Florida Marlins	2:36	Cincinnati Reds	1:64	Colorado Rockies	1:74
New York Mets	3:66	Houston Astros	2:72	Los Angeles Dodgers	3:28
Philadelphia Phillies	4:8	Milwaukee Brewers	3:48	San Diego Padres	4:40
Washington Nationals	5:30	Pittsburgh Pirates	4:14	San Francisco Giants	4:42
		St. Louis Cardinals	4:38		

About the Authors

James Buckley, Jr. is the author of more than 60 books for young readers on a wide variety of topics–but baseball is his favorite thing to write about. His books include *Eyewitness Baseball, The Visual Dictionary of Baseball, Obsessed with Baseball*, and biographies of top baseball players, including Lou Gehrig. Formerly with *Sports Illustrated* and NFL Publishing, James is the president of Shoreline Publishing Group, which produced these volumes. Favorite team: Boston Red Sox.

Ted Keith was a writer for *Sports Illustrated Kids* magazine and has written several sports biographies for young readers. Favorite team: New York Yankees.

David Fischer's work on sports has appeared in many national publications, including *The New York Times, Sports Illustrated*, and *Sports Illustrated Kids*. His books include *Sports of the Times* and *Greatest Sports Rivalries*. Favorite team: New York Yankees

Jim Gigliotti was a senior editor at NFL Publishing (but he really liked baseball better!). He has written several books for young readers on sports, and formerly worked for the Los Angeles Dodgers. Favorite team: San Francisco Giants.